Quick and Easy Book Writing

– Tips, Tricks and Time-Saving Information on How To Write A Book For The First Time

experience in the utilization of any of the ideas, techniques, or suggestions contained in this volume.

Terms of Use

With your purchase, you've been given a non-transferable, "personal use" license to this product. This means that there are absolutely no resell, reprint, duplication, or private label rights granted when purchasing this document. In other words, this copy is for your own personal use.

Thank you for respecting these terms. Now go ahead and enjoy your purchase and be sure put this information to work for you. I wish you the best!

Robert Boduch

Table of Contents

3

Introduction

Thank you for taking a leap forward in your life... and a leap of faith in trusting me to deliver the details that will help you write your book FAST. I vow to do whatever it takes to help you enjoy to prestige and profits that come from writing and self-publishing your own material.

Having a book of your own can pay off in so many ways.

For example, your authentic book is a reliable source of additional cash flow that comes to you automatically, every month. Write your book, publish it, get it in front of the people who can benefit most and you will earn a tidy sum from every single sale.

Your book positions you as an expert and allows you to charge more for your professional services and speaking gigs without a hitch. As an author, your market's perception of the value of your goods and services soars and resistance to your higher fees is rarely even a factor.

Your book speaks volumes about you. It's an excellent way to reach a growing audience every single month. It's a great way to introduce what you do to others and a book you can hold in your hands beats the traditional business card – hands down. As a lead generator, your book has the capacity to draw attention and interest on a global basis. As more people hear about you and learn more about your expertise, your credibility and respect in the marketplace increases also.

Self-publish your work and you can charge any price you choose. Or you can give it away to build a mailing list, spread the word about your services, or make a name for yourself. At any rate – you only have to do the work once. But the rewards can last a lifetime – and beyond.

For the beginner, writing a book can seem like a daunting task. That's why so few ever pull it off, although it's a popular lifetime goal that routinely shows up on surveys and lists. There are multiple steps and choices along the way.

While you could spend years writing a single book, it need not take you more than 30 days at the very most.

I've prepared this information to simplify the process for you. This publication will help you get your book written and on the market in a whole lot less time. I'm not talking about those lean publications many call "ebooks" – although they only contain 10 or 20 pages of questionable content.

What you're about to discover will help you craft a "real book" of some 100 - 200 pages – a book you can proudly hold in your hands and feel its substance. There's no reason why you can't sell it as a digital product too – in fact I encourage all my students to do so. But by writing a meaty volume that's loaded with tips, techniques and inside secrets – you set yourself and your readers up to win big time.

Let's get started.

Chapter One: 14 Good Reasons Why You Really Should Write Your Own Non-Fiction Book – And Do It NOW!

Reason #1: Anyone Can Do It

Let's clear up one myth right off the bat: book writing isn't the exclusive domain of the super-creative geniuses among us. It's something anyone – including you --can do, right here, right now.

It really doesn't matter who you are, or what you've been doing with your life up to this point in time. None of that matters in the grand scheme of things. If you sincerely want to write a book – you most certainly can. I'm living proof that anyone can jot down a few thoughts, turn it into a product and actually make money with it.

Almost everyone wishes they had a book to their credit. But far fewer have the desire and drive to make it happen. They'd like to be an author to enjoy the perks and profits -- but are unwilling to put in the time and write the necessary pages.

There is some definite work involved. No one is going to write your book for you, unless you pay them handsomely to do it. You've got to be willing to roll up your sleeves and bear down. But the purpose of this book is to simplify the process of writing a book so that literally anyone can do it a matter of days, instead of years.

It's not the absence of capability that prevents the majority of people from becoming authors, it's the absence of desire and belief that they can pull it off.

Fact is... you can get started today and complete your book in 30 days, or less -- sometimes a lot less. In my "One Hour Bestseller" report, I share some simple methods for creating informational report, ebooks and other products super-fast. These are much shorter than traditional books, of course. But it's a viable option to crank out a decent product on a Saturday afternoon.

 It really depends on the size of book you want to write and the methods you use to write it. I'm here to tell you that writing and selling your creation is a lot easier than you think. Over the course of this text, I'll prove it to you... beyond any shadow of doubt.

Writing a successful book means writing a book that sells. Let's be clear about that from the outset. If it doesn't sell well and put plenty of money in your pocket... what are you doing it for? Sure, there are other rewards like seeing your name as author on a colorful book cover. But that kind of euphoria doesn't last long, although it does give the ego a nice boost.

What will sustain both your pocketbook and your psyche for years to come are the continuous profits from your creation, month after month.

Reason #2: Non-Fiction Book Writing Has Several Advantages

My purpose is to give you every possible advantage to help you get your own best-selling book written and produced in the shortest possible time.

Since that's the objective, I strongly urge you to stay away from fiction writing – at least in the beginning. If that's the direction you ultimately want to go, fine. But if creating a solid book in as little time as possible and actually making money from it, I implore you to get started in the non-fiction arena.

Limitations are removed in non-fiction writing. There's no pre-requisite, no special qualifying that must take place if you are to succeed from the get-go. You can start right where you are... and create an outstanding book that makes you boatload of cash.

The simple key to non-fiction writing is to provide the information people want to know. Be the well that supplies the water and you'll have no shortage of eager buyers willing to shell out cash for the answers and detailed information you provide. We'll get into exactly how to do that a little later. For now, just keep in mind that there are thousands of specific markets with specific problems, just waiting to be solved. You can easily step in and become a force with your problem-solving book. You can make a significant contribution to others and a lot of money for yourself at the same time. It's a classic win-win situation.

Fiction writing is a harder nut to crack – at least in the traditional sense. Think about it for a moment. Who are the best-selling fiction writers? The likes of Steven King and J.K. Rowling are known names. Their books sell well because millions have come to know and love their work. But trying to break into that market could be challenging, though the winds of change are transforming the entire publishing industry and previously unknown authors like Amanda Hocking, John Locke and Stephen Leather and making it big as self-published fiction writers.

Selling fiction is speculative in nature. You write your story and hope that someone, somewhere likes it enough to publish you work. You could self-publish your work, but marketing an unknown fiction writer is can be a difficult task. That's not to say it's impossible – particularly in these exciting and unprecedented times.

I truly believe human beings are capable of anything they commit serious focus and attention towards. It's just that I like to have the deck stacked in my favor, with the best possible odds from the beginning. For the first-time author, non-fiction is more likely to be a safer bet and this is the route I urge you to take.

If you choose fiction, you had better be the resilient and persistent type. But if you want to dramatically improve your chances for success, stick with non-fiction and follow the ideas presented on these pages.

Reason #3: Writing Your Non-Fiction Book Is Easier Than You Think

Follow these ideas and you'll have your book completed in less time than you ever thought possible. Anyone can do it – they really can. There's really nothing to it, as you're about to see. You don't have to spend hours upon hours in isolation, away from your family and friends. Just break your book idea down into small, bite-size components and knock off one at a time.

Begin with step one and follow your plan of action through to the end. With the final step, you'll have your book completed sooner than you think.

Non-fiction writing is particularly easy to fit into a formula. Learn to spot details that work for others and follow these tried and true methods. It isn't exactly rocket science... though with your new book in hand, friends might assume you've acquired some special power from an unknown frontier.

Outline your work – that's key number one.

A quality outline makes for a quality book. Not only that, your outline makes the actual writing a wondrous joy as your fingers fly across the keyboard faster than they ever did before. It's a wonderful thing to witness and even better to participate in.

Key number two is to write in timed segments.

Chunk it down, section by section and piece by piece. Then with each segment, do nothing but write for 5, 7, 10 or even 20 minutes at a time.

When you limit the time spent on each individual segment, you train your brain to spit out the really good stuff immediately. There's no long-winded wind-up. No meaningless drivel. You don't waste any words in making your point. Instead, you'll find yourself getting right to the information that's most relevant and significant to the reader.

"Have something to say and say it as clearly as you can. This is the only secret to style." – Matthew Arnold

Finding your voice is easy when you challenge yourself with time-limited writing broken down into small, easily handled increments. Write enough (a few segments in succession) and your true voice emerges. When you reach this blissful state, the words flow effortlessly and continuously, making the act of writing a magical experience.

The only problem with this approach is that it may take you a page or two before you're warmed up and "in the zone" -- not exactly the most productive use of your time. It works best when you warm-up first. Answering email messages is a good way to get prepared for an hour or two of productive writing.

Personal productivity soars when you allow yourself freedom of voice within preset parameters. Unlimited freedom can quickly get you off track. But with just 7 minutes to cover a topic, you quickly adapt and write concise, to-the-point copy that is coherent and gets the job done in as few words as possible. Without this kind of framework in place, chances are you'll ramble on, or veer off course. When you've only got mere moments to deliver the goods – you tend to get right to it.

Reason #4: Make Money

Ahhhhh – sweet cash! Is there anything better? Oh sure, health, happiness and love are essential to a wonderful life. But lets' face it, in today's society you've got to have a certain amount of money to survive.... and to enjoy life to the fullest requires even more.

I honestly can't think of a better way for anyone of reasonable intelligence to consistently make good money than by writing books. Once your book is a done deal... actually, even before it's completed -- you can start to make money from it. Isn't life grand?

How much money can you make? Well, in self-publishing at least, the sky really is the limit. But how much money you actually generate depends on several factors including your chosen topic, market demand, and the effort you put forth towards marketing and promotion. Your incoming cash flow could be a trickle or a raging river... or a variation of both for many years to come. At any rate, having your own book on the market can pay you some exciting cash dividends.

How you actually get paid depends on the format of your production.

16

If you take the traditional publishing route, you'll likely receive a payment up front, and semi-annual or annual royalties from sales, typically 5% to 15%. This is of course after your book has been accepted by a publisher – no small feat in itself. With a successful book, you could generate passive income for several years. But an unsuccessful book taken on by a publisher might only last 30 to 60 days on store shelves. After that, your book is for all intents and purposes, finished.

With self-publishing, you make your money from every sale and all profits generated are yours to keep.

You'll make a lot more from each individual sale this way as you take care of your book's production and delivery and keep 100% of the revenues. With small print production runs and Print-On-Demand technology, you can keep costs to a manageable level, without investing in extra inventory. The result is a leaner operation and greater profitability.

As a general rule, I like to shoot for a minimum of $50,000 in earnings from each book I write. That's a nice target to aim for and reaching it pays me handsomely for every hour of effort I put forth. Keep in mind many successful self-published authors make a whole lot more than this from just one book they've written. But if my sales reach $50,000 to $100,000 -- I know writing the book has been a very worthwhile endeavor.

That's just one of the things I love about writing books. How many other "jobs" offer this kind of potential, working from the comfort of home, being immersed in a subject you're crazy about, without risking anything but your time? Fact is, you can earn a terrific income and give your cash flow a significant shot in the arm, at an absolute minimum risk.

Reason #5: You Can Predict Your Success In Advance

Choose your subject correctly, and you're on the fast track to success. Simply find a problem looking for a solution. That's it. Find the problem first... then create the best possible way to solve it in the form of a book. Do this and you've got a sure-fire winner and a certain profit center.

That's what makes non-fiction writing an absolute goldmine and the easiest option in which you can consistently produce books that sell again and again. Anyone can do it – seriously! The trick is to leverage your own personal experience, background and interests to create something of unique value.

All you have to do is identify a common or recurring problem. Learn to look for things that annoy, frustrate, stress-out, disappoint, or anger people. Identify the source of their pain. Then... develop a powerful antidote, remedy, or solution.

Spot the unmet "needs" and "wants" in the marketplace and satisfy them better than anyone else and you're well on your way. The more effective you are at selecting a market or niche – the more potential profit awaits you.

Predicting your success in advance is about finding topics with a high-probability of solid sales for months or years. Contrast this with the hit or miss nature of fictional books and you'll see why non-fiction is a much better option for most.

Non-fiction writing is a direct route to supplying precisely what the market desires. Writing in this genre is more science than art. You don't need to be especially creative to produce an outstanding book. Instead, what serves you well is a business-like approach where you simply provide what people are willing to pay for. Be the source of practical, useful information. It works for me – I know it will work for you too.

Reason #6: You've Got Information of Value

It's a goldmine... and you're sitting on it. It doesn't matter where you've been, what you've done in the past, or who you think you are as person. ***What you've done up until this point is experience life and the path you've taken is exclusively yours.*** No one else has walked in your shoes and tasted life quite the same way.

Precious information is stored in your memory. I'm here to tell you that the very same information you might take for granted is information that would help other people. My mission throughout this book is to help you identify and extract this information and shape it into a book that others will gladly pay money for. That's what it's all about – tapping into your inner resources to give people exactly what they want for a very nominal fee.

Somewhere along life's path, you faced a challenge and created or adapted your own unique solution.

Now it's your opportunity to share your discovery and make your contribution known to humankind. At some level within you lies valuable information -- information that can substantially improve life at some level for thousands -- even millions -- of others.

You may not have all the answers at this point, but I can assure you that you've already got a strong foundation for a powerful thesis. Bring it forward. Now it's just a matter of turning your time-saving, money-saving, stress-reducing, health-inducing, or otherwise effective "solution" into a format that can benefit buyers the world over.

19

To profit from your information, you must share it. Don't hoard it. Spread your insight, your wisdom and your discoveries and not only will you be helping others tremendously, but you can earn staggering profits too.

Reason #7: Writing Books Is the Ultimate Business Opportunity

Imagine enjoying the ultimate in freedom – where you can write whatever you want to write. Now take those pages of written material and transform them into a product... and you have unlimited earning potential.

Both the creation and marketing of your book can be exciting adventures. Write it once and profit from your words thousands of times over. That's the lifestyle of a successful self-published author... and it's one you can soon enjoy too.

Anything is possible. It's all within your grasp as an independent author. You work when you want... write about things that interest you... and sell your creations in dozens of countries around the world – all from the comfort of home. There are few other lifestyle options I know of that offer the kind of freedom a successful self-published author gets to enjoy every day.

I'm not saying that you'll make millions and live a life of leisure with the rich and famous by writing a single book. Nor am I saying this is impossible for you either. Others have done it. So there's no reason why you can't do the same.

But it's not my intention to feed you with false hope or set you up with unnecessarily high expectations. Realistically, if you follow these instructions and take action on your dreams, you can expect to earn at least a few thousand dollars. As an entrepreneurial-minded writer, there's no ceiling on your earnings, so you can earn as much or more than any salaried employee can working for the largest corporation if you stick with it and market your works effectively.

Once you begin reaping the rewards of your first book, you'll naturally want to write a follow-up. But this time around, you'll have cash flowing in from the sales of your first book, while your busy cranking out your second effort, making it easier still.

Few things inspire you to greatness more than receiving a whack of checks, direct deposits and credit card payments from locations thousands of miles away. While working on my second book, I received orders for my first, from such places as India, Denmark, Russia, Paraguay, and South Africa. For an unknown beginner from suburban Toronto -- this was exciting news!

I write my books in English, so it's no surprise that most sales have traditionally come from customers the United States, Australia, New Zealand, United Kingdom and Canada. But periodically a new order comes in from less likely place like Norway, or Nepal, or Turkey and I must say, it's thrilling when it happens.

Selling your work brings a deep sense of inner satisfaction. Writing a book that interests someone enough to actually pay you money in exchange for your thoughts is a gratifying experience. It's a beautiful thing – whenever it happens. You'll never grow tired of it and every sale you make will inspire and encourage you to even greater accomplishments.

Another terrific advantage of being an author is the valuable feedback you get from buyers.

When you've got your head buried in a stack of research material -- stopping only to check your email – only to discover a comment like *"I just wanted to write you a quick note to say what a terrific book you've written. It's absolutely fantastic!"* it fuels you to carry on. You find renewed energy and spirit to keep at it -- just to get your next project completed. Such commentary can help you through the tough times, whenever your project hits a snag, so keep all your positive feedback and read them again when you need an emotional boost.

Reason #8: It's A Low-Cost Business to Start and Operate

With your own book-writing venture, you can work at your own pace, part-time or full-time. There's no boss breathing down your neck and no office politics either. It's just you, your pen, notebook and computer.

There's no inventory to buy and stock... no special equipment or vehicles to purchase or lease... no signs to erect... and no office, warehouse, or shop facilities to rent. You work from a quiet corner of your home – on your own terms.

It's incredibly easy to get started. All it really takes is the decision to do so. You don't need a separate business bank account. Nor do you need any special permits or licenses, since you won't be making excessive noise, drawing crowds to a residential neighborhood, or using any hazardous material.

All you really need is a pad of paper and pen. What could be easier? A computer is a terrific tool for making the writer's life easier -- but the truth is, it's not absolutely essential to get started in the writing business. Make getting your own laptop or desktop computer a priority. But don't put off starting your book because of it.

You may be wondering what all this "starting a business" talk is about. After all, this volume is about writing a book, not launching a home-based business. But since you'll be creating a product and likely marketing it on your own, you're essentially "in business" for yourself.

Don't worry if you don't consider yourself a savvy businessperson. This book will give you all the tools you need to launch your own successful income generator. Plus, you'll be given additional tips and resources to further your marketing knowledge and skills.

I don't think there's another career path that offers such a huge potential reward and unlimited freedom -- at virtually zero cost and no risk whatsoever. You can start from wherever you are today and within the next 30 days - you could have a finished manuscript in hand. Just think of the power this gives you. It's something that can transform your life – just as it's done for thousands of other authors.

Reason #9: A Book is a Superb Marketing Tool

Whatever it is you do for a living, don't you think having your own book would be a definite asset to your career? Write about your professional specialty and you've gained a distinction over everyone else in the industry.

Think about it.

Before, you were an accountant, customer service consultant, interior designer, or _____ (fill in the blank). With your own book, you're no longer on the same playing field as countless others -- now you're not just an accountant, but also the author of *101 Little-Known Tax-Reduction Secrets for Business Owners.*

If this was you, and you were competing with hundreds of other accountants for the same customers, wouldn't this give you a decided advantage in the marketplace? You bet it would! Becoming an author is a distinction that gives you a decided advantage. You're no longer on par with everybody else. You're now a "specialist" and an "expert". That's the perception at least. **It's how the world and more importantly – your marketplace – sees you.**

An interior designer could do the same thing to quickly establish a level of heightened perception in the marketplace. Imagine showcasing your work and explaining the thinking behind it.

Any business owner could write a book and use it to diversify his or her existing business. Consider the ways a book might help your current customers. While shopping for a gift for my father-in-law (a committed pipe smoker and all-around handyman) I stumbled upon the pimopipecraft.com website. This site sells everything you could ever need to create fully functional pipes. Their selection includes chunks of briar, various pipe stems, specialty drill bits, and jigs – and most importantly a book – *Pipe Crafting at Home*. I'm sure this company sells plenty of books. Not only is it a natural add-on to the various specialty supplies they carry, it's an essential resource for the first time pipe maker.

The key to this approach is to make your book a complimentary addition to your product line. Make it something customers can't find anywhere else. This gives you an additional product that costs little to produce, but provides the much needed answers customers seek, while generating additional revenues for your business.

Regardless of your chosen field, there's a tremendous opportunity awaiting you to create a distinct and powerful advantage for yourself -- and attract more prospects, customers, sales and cash flow as a result.

Your book gives you an enhanced position in the marketplace. You gain instant credibility and elevate yourself several steps up the expertise ladder. The distinction of having written a book in your area of specialty gives you a more prominent standing – one that definitely opens more doors.

A book is a great source of new leads and customers. It's a way of reaching people who may want your products and services, but who otherwise never would have heard of you. Any professional, independent sales-person, or business owner can create a book that pulls in more prospects and customers directly. But what if you don't work for yourself? Can you still profit from your occupational expertise? Yes you can.

Suppose you're a customer service representative in a large firm. You're a master at putting out fires and smoothing over the rough spots to make the customer's experience a pleasant one. You could write a training manual for customer service reps, showing them the simple but effective techniques you've evolved over the years. It may be second nature to you... but a serious challenge for others.

Not only would such a book be useful to other would-be customer service people directly, corporations may be interested in bulk quantities as part of their internal training packages.

Consider the added clout authorship gives you in seeking a new position, or negotiating a raise. Again, having written a book will have boosted your PPV – *Personal Perceived Value.*

Using your professional expertise is just one approach to book writing. It's a great way to increase your exposure and income. In terms of sheer marketing value, your own book is tough to beat.

Reason #10: Build or Enhance Your Reputation

Getting your book written and out in the marketplace gives you widespread exposure. You'll connect with people you couldn't possibly reach any other way. More than likely, you'll generate orders from remote areas of the world you hadn't heard much about since your elementary school days. The cumulative effect is a rising reputation and increased name recognition.

Once you've officially become an "author", you're automatically elevated in the minds of others. It's a plateau that's highly esteemed. You gain new status as your name becomes more widely recognized and by osmosis, your reputation is enhanced.

Increased visibility exposes your name and material to a wider audience, so more people find out about you and your particular level of skill and expertise. Greater exposure means increased market visibility.

Writing a book adds to your credentials. Authorship raises your community profile and perceived value. No longer are you simply the owner of a travel agency specializing in African safaris – you actually wrote the book on it. Cool!

Imagine being a chef in a quality restaurant. Want to explode your restaurant's popularity and enhance your own reputation at the same time? Write a book. Share a piece of your magic and spread the word about your culinary expertise through the printed word.

You could do this with any business... any profession... any career – even a hobby. Write your book and you'll see for yourself. It's a terrific way to get a leg up on the competition.

Reason #11: You'll Gain Self Confidence

Get your book written and published and watch your self-confidence skyrocket. No matter how you slice it, writing a book is a wonderful accomplishment. It's a major undertaking, or so it seems to most people.

Overwhelmingly, the majority figure writing a book is such a gigantic project that it could easily take at least a year or two just to pull it off. That's one of the major reasons most people never get around to writing a book in t he first place.

But armed with these speed-writing secrets, you'll knock off your full-size book in 30 days or less by following these ideas and chipping away at it, bit-by-bit. The resulting effect is your self-confidence will soar in a fraction of the time... and no one will ever know you kicked your book out in a matter of days instead of years.

Despite the fact that you'll get it done in a fraction of the time, you'll still enjoy a richly satisfying sense of accomplishment. Your book will be every bit as good -- if not better -- than the book that takes another writer 3 full years to finish. You'll discover inner qualities and abilities you didn't realize you had and give your self esteem a significant lift in the process.

Helping others is inherently fulfilling. It satisfies the soul. Your book is a way of reaching many people from various countries around the world. These are people who might not otherwise ever have the chance to learn from you and tap into your wisdom.

Zig Ziglar, the famous sales trainer, motivational speaker and author once said...

"Help enough other people get what they want, and they'll help you get what you want."

Personal experience shows that the more people you help --
the more you'll hear about it and the more you'll ultimately
profit. Give people the information they really want and they
feel compelled to express their gratitude. The fact that you
make more money by helping more people could almost be
considered a secondary benefit of writing your book.

The accolades and recognition by others is a rewarding form
of payment in itself. You'll beam with newfound pride at your
wonderful creation and you'll be amazed at what you've
accomplished in such a short period of time.

More prospects, more customers, more contacts and more
cash will begin flowing your way. Others will actively seek
you out, hold you in high regard and value your ideas and
opinions on various topics – not only the one you've just
written about. Suddenly you're in demand as more
opportunities appear simply as a result of your book.

Chances are you'll never be the same again. Like the butterfly
emerging from the cocoon, you'll have outgrown your old
self.

The result is a new, better-known, more prosperous and
confident you. It's a transformation in personal growth that
makes your book writing project well worth the effort –
whether you ultimately sell 100 copies... or 5,000,000 in 17
different languages.

Reason #12: You Gain Recognition and Respect

Almost everyone would like to have a book to their credit...
but few rarely reach this pinnacle of success. Perhaps that's
one of the reasons why authors are respected in our society.

With your finished book completed and available to others, you'll start making a name for yourself. You'll get noticed for your ideas and expertise and increased opportunities will naturally gravitate towards you. That's just the way it works.

If you write about your business, industry, or profession, your insights are exposed for all your market to see. What better way for others to gain a glimpse into who you are and what valuable insights you bring to the table?

Your book places you front and center. It boosts your image, value and positioning amongst your peers. It means you're serious about what you do and it helps people remember who you are. After all, you're the guy (or gal) who wrote the book on the subject.

The result is that more people, money and opportunities tend to appear and with much greater frequency. You're an author now – a "somebody" in the eyes of your marketplace or community. You may have been a VIP in your own mind before, but now others see you this way. They respect you as an authority – an insider – and in the marketplace where the ultimate opinion is expressed by spending money, perception is everything.

Reason #13: You Only Have To Create It Once... and You Profit for Years

Imagine a never-ending payday from a single month of work. This kind of long-term reward is common for a carefully selected, non-fiction book that solves a troubling problem, or fulfills an unsatisfied desire. It can certainly happen for you as it's happened for me.

My first book-writing effort was a short, 75-page publication I created back in 1996. Though its best days are long gone, this book still generates a few sales and some extra cash each and every month. The crazy thing is that I've consistently made money from this "evergreen" book month after month and year after year without ever significantly changing or upgrading the original text. Maybe it's time to rewrite, refresh and re-launch a new edition.

The money this book brings in these days is hardly enough to retire on in Bermuda, but it's nice to continually cash in on work I once did, long, long ago. Think about that for a moment. A single writing effort can continue to pay off for you -- even many years down the road. That's the power you hold in your hands.

I've discovered plenty about writing and selling books since those early days. If you follow these ideas and learn from my experience, I promise you a windfall that will dwarf my first book writing experience.

Start looking for problems. Seek out a specific problem that an identifiable group of people want to solve badly. Do so and you'll be rewarded. People who are hungry for a solution will gladly pay you for yours.

Develop a solution in a way that can continue to serve others who experience the same type of problems. It's not enough to create a book of plans for an alcohol still as an alternate fuel source due to a temporary oil shortage caused by a crisis in the Middle East, or political maneuvering at OPEC. So far at least, these situations have proven to be only temporary. As prices stabilize, the market for such a book tends to evaporate quickly.

You might get lucky and cash in quick. But you're probably better off to write about "evergreen" subjects that sell well year-round, with no expiry date just beyond the horizon.

Look for widespread desires you can help fulfill. Wanting more out of life is a universal desire.

Help people discover themselves, their innate inner qualities. Show them how to improve their own skills quickly and easily. How can you help them grow professionally... socially... or physically? This is the kind of information many hunger for and it's something you can easily supply.

Creating your book once and profiting from it for years is the ultimate in leverage – a fundamental business concept of producing **maximum returns for minimum effort expended.** Contrast this with the typical work life of an employee.

Imagine a letter carrier, if you will. She rises in the morning, reports to work and picks up her load of mail for the day. After a steady effort, the job is done and it's time to go home. But then the next day, there's a fresh new load of mail just waiting to be delivered.

At the end of each pay period, this employee receives pay, based on the number of hours or days on the job. There's only so much money she can earn on the job, regardless of performance. Once maxed-out, that's as far as she can go. Most "jobs" are exactly the same. You're paid for your time on the job and nothing more.

What's great about writing books is that you can make ten, fifty, even one hundred times more money from the same number of hours in one pay period. Is this an exciting way to spend your time, or what? Your book delivers maximum return at minimum effort, expense, and hassle. It's about working smart... rather than working hard.

Make it a perennial best-seller and you could earn a tidy sum every year. You can upgrade your work periodically, if you wish, making it even more inviting with fresh new content. Or, you can basically leave it alone, as long as the ideas you share are timeless in nature.

Writing your book is surprisingly easy. I'm going to share my exact formula. All you have to do is follow it.

Reason #14: You Grow Immensely From the Experience

In case you're not yet sold on writing your book, I'm going to reveal another benefit – one that you'll need to experience in order to see. Writing your book can give you everything you want – both tangible and intangible.

At first, writing a 100+ page book might seem like a daunting task. That's just fine by most writers. They don't really want you to discover how easy it is. After all, writing a book is supposed to be a long, difficult, arduous task. It's not supposed to be the walk in the park it actually is. That's why when you write that final paragraph and your book is for all intents and purposes complete, you'll feel like a new person.

Let's face it... most people think writing a book is a monumental task. You probably do too. But knock off one chunk at a time and see it through. I guarantee you'll surprise yourself. You'll accomplish more than you ever thought possible and when all is said and done, you'll have grown immeasurably as an individual.

Writing your book is an opportunity to profit from information that's mostly stored within.

Choose a topic you know well and you'll be astonished at the material that flows from the recesses of your marvelous mind. Release the shackles and let your mind flow with ideas. Get it all out and get it down on paper.

Let others profit from your know-how. **The paradox is that the more you share, the more it comes back to you.** Give first and you'll receive plenty.

With your first book written, produced, and on the market, life begins taking you in new directions. Don't be scared by this natural evolution, just let the good times roll. It's a liberating experience. New opportunities will come to you. Some will be lucrative, others less so. Some may even be fraudulent, so you'll need to conduct due diligence before taking action. Write it and get your book out there. Then let all that life has to offer come your way.

It all starts with your first book. Chances are it won't be your last.

Chapter Two – What To Write About To Give Yourself the Highest-Probability of Success

Life Experience

Whatever road you've travelled, your journey is rich in experience. No one else has taken the exact same path you have. No one has seen, felt, heard, observed, endured, tasted, or otherwise "lived" the journey in the exact same fashion. Simply put, you are truly one of a kind.

Regardless of age, you've got years worth of life experiences under your belt. It's this "life experience" that fully qualifies you as a writer with an exclusive source of content.

Your path is your own. It's real... and it's uniquely yours. So when you write about personal experience, you're communicating from a vantage point no one else can duplicate 100%.

Along the way you've encountered many unique experiences, gained individual perspective, and learned lessons others haven't. It's all recorded, deep within your mind. Somewhere amidst all this recorded data lies opportunity – opportunity you can turn into a book and by extension, your own money tree.

Maybe as a student, you spent an entire summer hitch-hiking across the country – and lived to tell about it. You could write about your travels, the people you met and the places you got to visit on a shoestring – all from a travelling student's perspective.

Perhaps an early job in a pizza shop turned you into a gourmet pizza chef... or a successful restaurateur. You could write a cookbook... a passionate tale of pizza – past to present, or a business guide for aspiring pizza shop or restaurant owners.

It could be that your last job involved a huge project that required your specialized planning, organizing, implementation, and delivery expertise to get it done profitably for your company. Don't you think other managers, consultants and CEO's would love to discover your shortcuts, secrets and super-effective methods?

The trick is to match your internal information to a profitable opportunity.

Review your stored experiences and connect these to a marketplace problem in need of a solution. Chances are you know something others don't – something they'd gladly pay you for sharing.

It could be a recent experience or something from years ago. Dig it out. Dust it off. Examine it. Extrapolate the experience. Pretty soon you'll have a workable thesis defined for your book.

Re-visit even the negative experiences. You're not doing this to relive the pain – you're doing it to help other avoid experiencing the anguish you've already endured. The lessons you learned could help thousands of other people overcome their own similar problem or pitfall.

Barbara Ling used this concept in her book "Avoiding The Contractor From Hell". After surviving a disastrous renovation, the author recounted the experience in book form. It serves as a helpful warning to others about the various scams and potential pitfalls unscrupulous contractors try to pull. In the process, Barbara transformed a seriously negative situation into a positive outcome.

A recent example comes from Jaycee Dugard. Jaycee was kidnapped as a young girl and endured unspeakable acts of cruelty and brutality as she literally had her childhood stolen from her. Following her rescue and recovery, Jaycee wrote about her experiences in "A Stolen Life: A Memoir" and is now a bestselling author on Amazon and elsewhere.

You're Damn Good... At Something

It doesn't matter where you are in your life right now. It doesn't matter what you've done, the places you've been, or who you've become in the process. You are good enough at something to share what you know in words. In fact, it's likely that you're skilled at many things. The trick is to tap into that rich reservoir of skill, talent, knowledge, and ability within. Stop overlooking what you already have.

But if you're like most people, identifying the brilliance within is difficult. After all, you've probably taken it for granted... so it's not so obvious to you.

When you are able to identify those special attributes, you tend to downplay it, as though it's nothing special. Let me remind you that even though your own skills and knowledge may be second nature to you – that's NOT the case for everyone else you could impact. Hundreds, thousands, perhaps even millions want to know what you know – and they're willing to pay to glean your tips, techniques, insights and advice.

Tune in and turn on. Listen to those around you – they're usually quite effective at picking up on your golden attributes. Pay attention to the comments you receive – don't just brush them off.

36

If you keep hearing how unbelievably delicious your home-baked cookies, butter tarts, and berry pies are -- you've got skills and "inside knowledge" of value. Maybe it's time to write that book after all.

If friends regularly remark about the comfort and style of the rooms you've decorated, you've got a knack for interior design or home staging.

If you build custom furniture that wins rave reviews and your client waiting list is six months long, you're not just going through the motions – there's commitment, passion and no small amount of talent in your work. Share it.

Often it takes the acknowledgement of others to remind us of our own special skills, even though you may be instinctively aware on some level. The mere mention of it by others is validation. Pay attention and examine the marketability of your talents and knowledge in book format.

Awards & Recognition

Maybe you were a straight-A student through college – one of those who aced just about every assignment and exam, seemingly without effort. I bet you knew something others didn't... or had some unique reading or studying techniques that enabled you to focus on the critical information, while paying far less attention to the unimportant. Is this something others would like to know? Of course it is!

Maybe you won the regional championship three years straight as a little league baseball coach. If that's the case, you're a natural leader... you're great with kids... you understand the fundamentals of the game... and you know how to get the most out of people. That's 4 separate book ideas right there.

Tap into the value you already possess. It may be dormant –
but I assure you it's there. You have transferable knowledge.
All you need to do is shape it into a book that addresses the
desires of a definable group of prospective buyers. Hit upon a
large group of people and you've just found the key to the
vault.

Relive Past Memories

Peruse old photo albums. Review your childhood report
cards. Remember days of old and the things you've done at
various stages of your life. Capture the memories that flow
from those old snapshots. Talk to your parents, friends and
extended family about those days gone by. Relive the
moments and expand on the little things you uncover.

Think back to where you were 10 years ago. What did you do
with your time? Were you working full-time or part-time, or
were you in school? How is your life different now? What
were your other interests back then? **If you knew then
what you know now, how might your life be
different today?** What insights could you share with others
who are in the same position you were all those years ago?

Maybe you sold more Girl Guide Cookies than anyone else in
your group. What do you recall from the experience that
made you so successful? Relive your accomplishments and
you may uncover techniques you used that have helped
shape your direction and success today. There's value in such
hidden information and it's your job to peel back the layers.

Did reality force you to grow up at an earlier age? Maybe you
very cast in a role you didn't exactly plan for... but you pulled
it off brilliantly. What did you learn from the experience?
Write down whatever memories come to mind. Your past
could hold the key to a prosperous future. Take the time to
examine and explore as many possibilities as you can.

38

Notice Mistakes & Invent Solutions or Remedies

There's the "tried and true" approach... and then there's a better way. Just because a certain task has been done in a particular way for years, doesn't mean there isn't a viable alternative – one that's far superior. We're naturally creatures of habit, so we keep doing repetitive tasks until we (or somebody else) challenge the status quo and develop an improved method.

You probably said it yourself numerous times – "There's got to be a better way" – and if you said it, then it's a sure bet others have expressed those same sentiments too.

Now put your mind to work and create an improvement, or series of improvements that can be converted into a book. A sure-fire solution is one that simplifies the complex, eases the pain, makes life easier, or saves plenty of time or money – or both. In other words, **an effective solution solves a problem.**

Your solution-oriented book could be singular in nature such as, How To Double Your Child's Grades In School (Eugene Schwartz) or it could encompass numerous quick tips or fixes such as – 101 Ways To Save Money On Everyday Expenses.

Perhaps you've worked on a production line and can use your knowledge and experience to help others create "just-in-time" manufacturing solutions. Think that wouldn't interest anyone? Think again. I would have paid top dollar for this kind of information when I owned a small manufacturing company plagued by inefficient systems that cost me dearly.

"Cash flows to those who are able to solve people's pressing problems." -- Dr. Robert Anthony

Look for common or recurring problems... then create the ultimate solution.

Recently our garage was broken into and approximately $1500 worth of prized tools went missing in the middle of the night. The investigating officer said this kind of thing happens all the time and warned that I should expect a repeat visit sometime soon. This wasn't exactly the reassurance or comfort I sought. Anyone who has gone through similar experiences knows that insurance isn't the answer. Ultimately, it's the homeowner who has to do everything (within legal limits, of course) in his or her power to protect themselves against such losses.

Could you write a helpful book on do-it-yourself security for homeowners? If so, I'll be your first customer. What's more, if the police officer was correct in his assessment – there are loads of people in the same boat. Perhaps you could even get an insurance company to sponsor your project or at least buy a few thousand copies. After all... you'd be saving them a lot of money in insurance claims if people were better protected.

Keep your eyes peeled and opportunities will most definitely present themselves. Not happy with your child's progress in the school system? Why not research the alternatives including home-schooling, and provide this information in book format to other frustrated parents?

Book topics are everywhere – all you have to do is have a look around.

Everyday Teachers

Undiscovered opportunities might be sitting next to you at the dinner table. Look around at the people you see at different meals. Consider your family, friends, co-workers, business associates, club members, servers and those you meet on a regular basis. Many of these folks possess skills and specialized knowledge – something YOU could adapt into a marketable book.

Experts are everywhere. All you have to do is pay attention and you'll start to notice things.

A good place to start is within your own circle of influence. As an example, I could tap into my dad's ability for tinkering with electronic parts and gadgets and creating something that works – and write a book for other electronic enthusiasts. Or, I could recollect some of the conversations we've had about business, human potential, or the powers of the mind. There's plenty of usable material to draw from on each of these subjects.

My mom's baked pies are legendary. At a recent family gathering, the entire room suddenly fell silent – save for the occasional "Ahhhhh!" It wasn't due to any breaking news... or the big ball game playing on the television. It was mom's homemade apple pie being served – complete with a heaping scoop of French Vanilla Hagen-Daz. It's the kind of self-indulgence that demands one's full attention as each morsel is deliciously savored. You just can't talk and eat mom's apple pie at the same time. It's as though you'll cheat yourself out of the most amazing sensory experience of the holidays. Researching this one ought to be a lot of fun!

Brothers, sisters, cousins, nieces, nephews, grandparents – each can be a precious source of quality book material. It's just a matter of opening one's eyes and exploring the possibilities. I happen to come from a large family, so I've got a whole cast of characters to draw from. But this is something anyone can do. Just observe those around you.

Children are another excellent source of information. As adults it's easy to assume the role of teacher. But kids have a lot to teach us as well. Kids teach us about forgiveness,

41

unconditional love, having fun, and moving forward fearlessly. See any book ideas there?

What about your friends, business associates, or neighbors? My next-door neighbor is an auto mechanic. But he spends every bit of free time renovating, redecorating and otherwise adding value to his home. He's a natural at building decks, installing hot-tubs and knocking down walls to make way for a new patio door. He loves it... and saves tens of thousands of dollars every year. He'd be a terrific source should I ever write a book on Do-It-Yourself Home Renovating Like A Pro.

I bet that you're often in the presence of expertise too -- even though you may not recognize it. Look for passion, quality, commitment, and a caring attitude in the various activities of others.

Take note of all the people you meet, greet, or deal with on a frequent basis. There's the friendly variety store owner who has some great sources of low-cost wholesale products. He could be a rich resource of information for setting up a retail outlet or website, or to obtain low cost products for resale on eBay.

Then there's the fellow who owns the local bagel shop. Just last week he told me about his latest venture – taking over failed bagel shops from the banks who repossessed them. They know about his success and how easy he is to deal with.

The result is that he secures another money tree at a fraction of the price it would take to start from scratch.

The banks are happy as they recover part of their loss without any hassles. There are plenty of secrets here that others would be delighted to pay for in order to acquire and use themselves.

Special Events

Rare occasions present glorious opportunities. Have you ever taken an evening or weekend course taught by a legend? The Learning Annex used to be a fantastic local source of seminars and classes from top experts and authors from various areas of business, hobbies, and personal growth. If you've ever seen a Wayne Dyer or Les Brown live – you know how that it's a transformational experience. It's this kind of thing reawakening that can trigger a brilliant new topic idea.

Incidentally, The Learning Annex can still a source for hot topics, though they no longer run live classes – at least not in my area – although they do still operate online webinars. Look them up on Google and get on their mailing list and pay attention to the titles they promote. Any course taught there could be spun into a dozen or so different books. Back in the day these folks knew that the only way they would be able to fill seats was with at catalogue and website that was jam-packed with enticing titles and every issue had page after page of interesting classes listed.

Book sales work the same way. You need a killer title and subject to maximize results. I'll share much more about creating a great book title in a later chapter.

Here are just a few titles from a past issue of The Learning Annex catalogue:

- How To Get What You Want Out of Life
- Start A Profitable Online Retail Store
- How To Lose 7-15 Pounds Of Ugly Fat in Just 9 Days
- Get Published! Get Produced!
- How To Score Great PR For Yourself Or Your Business
- Make your Own Jewelry
- Pottery Making Techniques, Projects & Inspiration
- Become A Power Learner

- Law Of Attraction: How To Attract Anything or Anybody
- Look And Feel (Even Decades!) Younger
- Reiki: Awaken Your Healing Power Within
- How To Write Magazine Articles That Sell

Catalogues and course directories can prove to be an excellent source of ideas. At the very least, perusing these publications will stimulate your own creativity. Another big advantage is the timeliness of these courses. You'll discover topics that are hot right now.

Major Life Events and Chance Encounters

Have you ever had a life-altering experience? For some, it's a reprieve, a fresh new start from looming disaster. Perhaps your child was stricken with a serious disease. You dove into research mode, uncovering every bit of information you could on the subject and your child eventually made a full recovery. What you learned is more than enough to fill a book. Could you use that experience to help others?

Walking on fire was a life-altering experience for me. It transformed my belief about what was possible -- not just for me, but for humans in general. I learned to challenge conventional wisdom... to breakthrough my fears... and to push myself beyond anything I had done before. Although it happened years ago, I can vividly recall the magic I felt that night as though it was yesterday.

Approximately 500 others took the plunge that December evening and treaded slowly across a 12-foot long bed of white-hot coals that reached temperatures of 1200F. It was truly an unforgettable experience. Felt like I was on cloud nine for weeks after. I wish you could experience these feelings too. Then you'd be absolutely convinced that writing your book is something you could easily accomplish. Should I ever write about challenging beliefs, I'll be sure to relive that special event that changed me forever.

Last summer I happened upon a visual display that again challenged my accepted beliefs. While touring one of the buildings at the Canadian National Exhibition, I noticed an artist busy at work. He didn't work with conventional tools, nor did he produce typical works of art. What this man, Daryl Maddeaux, did was create "impossible" visual displays by stacking rocks of all sizes and shapes vertically.

It was an impressive display. He'd begin on the floor and create art by stacking seemingly impossible combinations of rocks up to six or seven feet in the air. When you witness this kind of thing, it changes you. Your established beliefs are challenged and it makes you wonder what else is possible for human beings to accomplish.

Life's Lessons

There are lessons to be learned and great subjects just waiting to be written from those daily lessons we encounter in our everyday lives.

Important lessons from humans, animals and nature remain to be unearthed and shared. Each source offers valuable fodder for the aspiring book writer. There is fantastic information just waiting to be shared.

Are you close to someone who has overcome great odds in accomplishing something? Maybe your friend was diagnosed with a serious illness, but failed to accept the verdict. Perhaps they took a road less traveled and survived. A documentation of their journey would offer comfort, encouragement and precious hope to many other similarly-afflicted patients and their families.

Peggy McColl wrote "Being a Dog With a Bone". It's a book that creatively draws upon dog analogies to teach valuable "life lessons", while inspiring readers to turn their dreams into reality. What lessons could you glean from pets at home, or animals in the wild? Could you transform those observations into a book? If you can map out a rough one-page outline, you can write a book.

Nature itself has much to teach us. Perhaps astronomy is your passion and you talk about it with other enthusiasts at every opportunity. Why not share your knowledge in print?

Do you enjoy gardening? Why not record all your "inside secrets" about safe, organic gardening methods and share your insights with the world?

Maybe hiking is your thing and you can wait to locate and explore new hiking trails. You could compile your discoveries, add brief descriptions and commentary on each, and bingo – you've got a topic – and you're off and running.

Past, Present, Future

Go back in time and relive more past memories. Take the "rocking chair" test. Imagine being 100 years of age and sitting back in your rocking chair, reviewing your life.

Reflect on the challenges, obstacles and opportunities you faced over your lifetime. What if you knew back then what you know now? What insights and information have you gathered over the years that others would be delighted to get their hands on?

Perhaps you struggled as a student, but as a businessperson you learned speed-reading techniques as a matter of survival in the fast-paced, dog-eat-dog world of big business. You know in your heart that you could have excelled in school if you were half as effective at reading as you are now. Ka-ching! There's your topic and a specific market that may be worth targeting.

Look at present conditions. What's missing in life for many people?

Today, we seem to have so much more than our parents or grandparents ever did. But are we any happier? For many, I suspect the answer is "no". They may have more "stuff" but they're not any happier. Why? Sorry, I don't have the answer to that one. But I do know that most people are "time poor" today and stressed-out more than ever before. Help alleviate these underlying problems and you could be providing an outstanding service to mankind through your book.

Predict the future. Take your crystal ball in hand and try to imagine what life will be like on our planet in the not too distant future.

Anticipate the coming changes. Observe changing demographics and "future-forward" how the inevitable might change things. Life sails by far too quickly for most of us. So helping people create the future they want by avoiding past mistakes is a popular general topic. That's something David Bach has done with his book, The Automatic Millionaire: A Powerful One-Step Plan to Live and Finish Rich.

Jobs, Careers, Training

What kind of work have you done in your life? You might have been employed as a waiter on a cruise ship and it gave you the opportunity to see various countries in Latin America or the Caribbean. Couldn't you help others do the same thing by writing about your experiences?

Maybe you were exposed to valuable training few others ever have the opportunity to take. Perhaps you served in the military and your specialized training makes you an exceptional leader, trainer, or motivator.

This is exactly the background author Jack Schropp drew upon when writing -- Unbeatable: Recreate Your Life As Extraordinary Using The Secrets Of a Navy SEAL.

I would guess that somewhere along the line you gained rare insights, received specialized trained, or otherwise acquired valuable inside knowledge about a particular field of endeavor.

Maybe this is just a start... but it's one worth exploring. Go back and take a closer look at all the training you've had over the years and begin to connect the dots. Consider training possibilities as book topics.

Better, Faster, Easier, Cheaper

People are always looking to improve their quality of life. They want to do more of the things they enjoy... and spend less time on those tasks they dislike. They want to discover improved methods and techniques for getting more of a return for less cost and effort.

"Better" means improvement over existing options, conditions, or circumstances. "Faster" helps people reach their objectives in less time. "Easier" allows the reader to get what they want more conveniently and with less effort. Help them do it for considerably less money and you'll have a bright, shiny carrot to dangle before their eyes and a potential bestselling topic in your hands.

Instant gratification is in hot demand. With an ever-increasing list of daily tasks and options competing for your reader's time, there's not much left to cater to the fulfillment of specific, personal "wants". Help you reader accomplish something in markedly less time and you'll attract definite attention.

Take a look at situations that frustrate people. Ever needed a lawyer who could do the job quickly, effectively, and affordably? Ted Nicholas spotted at this universal challenge and wrote – How To Do Your Own Legal Work.

After a tough day at the office, the last thing most people want to worry about is cooking a healthy meal. Yet, this is one of the things they need most to restore their worn out body and mind. How about a book on Healthy Home-Cooked Dinners in 10 Minutes or Less?

Chapter Three: 13 Big Mistakes That Stop Most People From Ever Completing Their Book... and How To Easily Avoid or Overcome These Blunders Every Time

Self-Sabotage

The biggest obstacle to your success in writing your book is... **you**. You could have an outstanding idea for a book and the ideal background for your subject, yet still manage to talk yourself out of writing it.

You could spend hours doing research... creating an extensive outline... even writing numerous chapters... only to run up against a self-imposed brick wall. When it comes to writing books (or going for big goals in life) it's quite possible that you are your own worst enemy.

It isn't that you don't want to experience the joy of success and every wonderful thing that comes with being a published author -- it's that on some level, you're preventing your own achievement from happening. Maybe it's a fear of failure... or even a fear of success.

Is there an author out there who didn't at some point worry about their effort being a total flop? I highly doubt it. Do your homework and take the necessary actions and your odds of failing are significantly reduced. Even if your book sales crash and burn during your initial efforts, you'll still get tremendous value from the creation process and you'll hold a useful asset that can be repurposed many different ways.

Locate an existing problem experienced by an identifiable niche market. Find ways to affordably connect with these people so you can share your important information. Create a book of viable solutions that produce tangible results way beyond anything they're currently experiencing. Do this and your chance of "failure" is so small, it doesn't even show up on the scale.

Some people work for months – even years – on their books but never seem to finish them off and get them out into the marketplace. They don't make it a high enough priority – or something else gets in the way.

The fear of success can be equally effective in holding you back from the life-changing opportunities you could enjoy by sharing your book with the world.

If you've struggled to get your book finished, it could be the fear of success that's preventing you from moving forward beyond a certain point. Unconsciously, you don't feel worthy or comfortable with the success that's within your grasp. It could be that you've never before written so much as a grocery list -- and now you're trying to write a book. The result is internal conflict between the conscious and sub-conscious mind. Like a tug-of-war, these opposing forces pull you in opposite directions, ensuring your book never sees the light of day.

Consciously, the would-be author wants desperately to finish. But it's all new territory. So the subconscious in an attempt to avert the pain of "failure" prevents it from happening.

The trick is to get the conscious and subconscious working in harmony. Do this and there's no inside "push and pull" – no internal conflict to sabotage your efforts. Your conscious desires are in alignment with who you are.

Visualize Your Results

To achieve internal harmony, create your results in advance. Establish the outcome first. Set a goal of having your book completed 30 days from now. Make it something you simply must accomplish. There's no turning back. No wandering. No making excuses. With this kind of commitment, there's no way you can fail. Your book will be completed by your chosen date and that's all there is to it.

Create a mock up of the cover and then visualize your completed book in your hands. See it in your mind's eye as a beautiful creation – something you can be proud of. Get a sense of how your published book looks and feels. Imagine the scent of a brand new book just delivered – but this one has your name on the cover as the author. Imagine the accolades and positive reviews as they come streaming in. Hear the words of your buyers expressing heartfelt gratitude for your outstanding work.

Replay this sensory-rich image in your mind over and over again and you'll soon have exactly what you imagined. I guarantee it. Create the scenario in advance... and then challenge reality to catch up. Accept yourself as an author and see your book coming together right on schedule.

Create your mental image exactly as you want it. Make it as real as possible. Set the mental prototype of your soon to be finished product. Do so and any obstacles can be quickly washed away. Creating an imaginary outcome and claiming ownership in advance is a time-tested secret to success. Accept nothing less and it's a done deal.

Distractions Can Be Deadly

Set out to achieve a new goal like writing a book and I can promise you one thing – distractions and obstacles will surface along the way. The trick is to expect these in advance. Know that disruptions are likely to occur and then deal with them as you would an unexpected visitor at your door. Simply handle the distraction, refocus and move on. Don't linger too long or you might find it too difficult to get back to work.

Distractions come in many forms and vary on the scale in terms of importance. It's the interruptive phone call, drop-in visitor, dental appointment, or unexpected family emergency that requires your immediate attention.

Some interruptions can be dealt with immediately, while others may take hours out of your day. Don't allow yourself to get off track and too far removed from your book project. Deal with the issues, events and interruptions as they occur and then get back to the task of writing your book.

Don't cheat yourself out of all the rewards your book can bring. Vow to press on no matter what. Work on your book everyday... even when you don't feel like it. Just do something that will move you one small step closer. Chip away at it. Stay the course and the reward will ultimately be yours. There is no other way.

Sharing Your Ideas With Others

Be careful here. Even revealing your ideas with close confidants can be self-defeating. In my experience, it's okay to share the occasional generality about your book. But do so with the utmost caution.

53

Your goal is to bring your book to fruition. Create a finished product... get it to market... and generate direct sales or use it as a lead-generator to build your business. Anything that could potentially get in the way should be avoided, if at all possible.

Reveal your "secret project" and it can quickly lose its power. It's like a hurricane -- incredibly powerful in the middle of the ocean -- but further inland, it often turns into nothing more than drizzle. Reveal too much about your goal and its power and luster quickly dissipates.

Keep your book project to yourself as much as possible – for as long as possible. Cross the threshold of disclosure when there's no turning back -- when it's just a matter of segments, or hours until your book is 100% complete.

At this point, it's much safer to open up a little and reveal more about your book. But only do so when you know in your heart that it's a done deal and nothing is going to stop you from finishing.

Some people tend to thrive on "constructive" criticism, but many are paralyzed by it, feeling that they've somehow made a fatal error. If you're not absolutely sure the feedback you receive won't stop you in your tracks – simply don't divulge any information. Get your book written first – then you can tell the world all about it.

With a completed manuscript in hand, you've got something of genuine value. You can always add to it, revise, modify, or otherwise polish it up. But I strongly urge you to just get it done first and adjust it later. Follow these proven steps to successful book writing and even the most rudimentary draft you create can eventually trigger an avalanche of cash flow for years to come.

Keeping your book a complete secret is difficult at the best of times. Unless you live on a deserted island, odds are someone is going to hear about your project long before its completion. How you react to the feedback you receive – solicited or not – is really up to you. It's not what people say, but how you respond, not in the heat of the moment, but over the course of the entire project. It's not what's given to you, but what you make of it. Never forget that.

Keep in mind that what any one individual has to say is merely an opinion – positive of negative. It need not become your reality. Well-intentioned or not, it can create unnecessary barriers that get in the way of your progression towards the finish line. Stay focused on your outcome and stick with it until you've written your book.

Don't take it personally if someone laughs at your idea or tries to poke holes in your plan. They may not realize, or even care about the damaging effects. The best insurance is to keep your ideas to yourself. Failing that, acknowledge the feedback... examine it and consider the source. Then decide if it's useless trash or unrecognized treasure. In any case, take whatever you get as a green light forward, rather than a stop sign.

Taking Too Long To Finish

As with any large scale project, writing a book requires concentrated effort. But how long are you willing to persist before something else demands your focus and attention? If it takes too long to do... let's face it... your book may never get done. Such is the reality of human nature.

That's why the sooner you can polish it off, the better.

If it takes a year, you'll have to deal with plenty of distractions. If you can do it in 90 days, you'll effectively wipe out 75% of those competing influences... and you'll profit from your book that much sooner. But in reality, 90 days is probably too long for most people.

If you really want to maximize your return on the time invested and realistically capitalize on your work in the shortest possible time – I suggest a 30-day book-creation period.

30 days is very realistic – even for a full-size book. It's an achievable goal for most people. Yes, it does require both a detailed outline and daily action steps to see it through. But you can certainly complete your book in 30 days – even in your spare time.

Can you write a book in less time? Certainly! It all depends on your current subject knowledge, personal schedule, your level of commitment and the size of your book project. Realistically, you could spend years writing a 200-page book. Or, you could invest as little as an hour or two to create a 30-page report or ebook using the methods as I share in The One Hour Bestseller or another approach. But you could also write that 200-pager in a whole lot less time if you roll up your sleeves and press on.

I encourage you to bang out your book in the next month. Do it in 30 days and you'll be elated with your accomplishment – especially if it continues to pay off financially for many years to come.

Take longer than 30 days and the chances of finishing your book begin to diminish. The longer it goes, the less likely it is you'll pull it off at all.

Once you've identified your hot topic, get to work on it at once. Plan your work then work your plan.

Zero in on the goal – the successful completion of your book. Get creative and let whatever related concepts, examples and details rise to the surface. Formulate your outline to simplify the writing phase of your project. With your detailed outline in hand, it's time to get started writing and create each segment as quickly as you can.

Write one segment at a time.

Then move on to another segment. Knock off 10 or 20 of these individual components and you've written another chapter of your book. But don't stop there – keep moving. Do so and you will get it done in less time than you expect. Develop what motivational speaker Brian Tracy calls a bias for action.

It's Already Been Done

Odds are that your brilliant idea has already been considered by someone, somewhere on the planet. In fact, there may already be hundreds of other titles written about your general topic. If you try hard enough, you can find plenty of competition in virtually any category. This is enough of a deterrent for some writers to cause them to abandon ship. But don't let the mere presence of related titles stop you.

Other books in your category merely indicate market interest. That's a good thing. If you're breaking new ground as a pioneer, you'll likely face additional challenges in the marketing of your book.

Obviously your book needs to be unique and advantageous to readers in order to sell thousands of copies. But if you focus on helping your reader overcome a challenge or solve a particular problem, you're doing a noble service and the market will show their appreciation by purchasing your product if it's made available to them.

Even in subject categories where you can find no direct competition, that doesn't mean somebody else isn't working on the exact same thing as you are. I made this discovery myself after writing my book on headlines. At the time I wrote it, I couldn't find anyone else with a book strictly about headline writing. But almost at the same time as my book was released, another copywriter released his own book on headlines too.

The truth is that there is room for both books. I've done very well with mine and I'm sure the other writer did so too.

Take any two books on an identical subject – and you'll find two completely different interpretations and presentations. This is as it should be. It does nobody any good to duplicate what's already out there. So just because some has already covered your topic doesn't mean that you can't still write your book and sell thousands of copies.

This very obstacle almost prevented this book from being written. I happened to mention the working title to an online friend. My friend mentioned another book released earlier that sounded exactly the same as the one I wanted to write. The problem was compounded by my friend's assertion that the other book was an "excellent" piece of work. I got the feeling that perhaps I was up against the wall and didn't stand a chance against what she termed "pretty stiff competition".

It was devastating news at first. I walked around dazed and confused for the next 24 hours. Then, I discussed this with my friend and she helped revise my perspective and move the project forward nonetheless. A couple of weeks later, it was done.

I concluded that since I hadn't read the other book, I couldn't say with certainty what information it contained. But the fact is, even if this book's concept was identical to the other author's – the two publications would be totally different works.

I venture to guess that this would be the case even if both parties had identical outlines to follow, since each writer draws from a unique perspective and experience. No two books are exactly alike, unless one writer deliberately copied another. (Not a particularly bright thing to do... but one that sadly can and does happen occasionally.)

If you're worried about another book on store shelves, sold online, or even a work in progress, you're probably focusing on the wrong thing.

You have no control over what another writer creates. So, why worry about it? Just point your concentration towards writing the best book of which you're capable. Give it all you've got and forget about the others. If your stew about the competition, real or perceived, current or future, you're wasting precious energy – and that energy is always better spent getting your book written and produced.

Take your raw material and add your unique and individual spin. Proceed confidently, secure in the belief that you're advancing a segment of society by sharing your ideas. So don't get allow yourself to get sidetracked into thinking you're wasting your time. You know in your heart the information you have to share is wanted and appreciated. So stay the course and continue you progress until your book is complete.

Never Getting Around To Starting

If you don't get started... there's only one possible result: failure. Sadly, is this fate that is handed to a lot of stellar concepts that could have been turned into amazing books.

But those volumes were never written because the would-be author didn't get started. I once heard speaker Bob Proctor say "Don't go to your grave with the music still in you."

Unfortunately this is exactly what happens to anyone who's ever said "I ought to write a book someday" and never followed through.

Until you make it a major priority in your life, your book is nothing more than a wish – a wish without any real power behind it.

Why not make someday, today?

You can do it! Writing a book is well within the realm of possibility for almost anyone. The longer you put it off, the more likely it is you'll never get it written. We all know too well how quickly life passes by... and the older you get, the faster it sails on.

Act on your ideas as they come to you. Jot them down, then later the same evening, pull out your notebook and examine the idea a little. Create a simple mind map as you explore and it will soon become apparent if your idea is full of potential and calling out to you. That's a clue – a clue you need to act on.

Start the ball rolling and you'll gain momentum on your project. But don't cast it aside for a later date. If you do, you can rest assured that someone else will pick up your golden concept and run with it. Wouldn't you rather be first up to bat? Being first gives you a decided advantage over all others.

Thinking too much about all that's involved in getting your book done will only cause you to keep putting it off.

The problem is that you and I are here to experience each moment as it is given. The harsh reality is that tomorrow may never come. Hopefully it will, but you never know for sure until it's here. The only absolute certainty is this very moment – right here, right now. You get one kick at it... and then it's gone for good.

Just get started on your book and keep at it. Take regular action and you'll never regret for one second your decision to write your own book.

Getting Started and Then Stalling Along the Way

Working on multiple projects simultaneously increases the possibility your book will at some point, be put on hold. Don't let this to happen to you.

Stay focused. Work towards accomplishing your goal of having your book completed by your chosen date. Make it your most important priority and you'll get it done. Treat it as a part-time thing and you'll only contribute content when the spirit moves you. This approach pretty much ensures you'll never reap the rewards of success as an author.

Focus is the key. Famous author and self-help expert, Wayne Dyer observed, *"Whatever you focus on expands"* and this has certainly been true in my experience. Make the completion of your book more important than virtually any other task you're faced with over the next 30 days. **Be firm, strict and deadly serious about this.** Think about the benefits you'll get to enjoy when your self-published book becomes a bestseller.

Do this and two things will happen…

1) You'll find renewed energy enthusiasm as you look for additional opportunities to take another step towards the completion or your book…

2) Information, ideas, contacts, opportunities, and chance encounters will naturally come to you in greater abundance. The more focused you are, the greater the flow of people, information, ideas and resources towards you. That's just the way it works.

Don't be spooked by this. Consider it as the universe assisting you in the fulfillment of your objective. The more you stay focused on your book, the easier it is to get it done. You'll feel a renewed sense of energy and vitality whenever you sit down to write and the closer you are to the finish line, the more exciting it gets!

Starting To Write Before Your Outline Is Complete

Wondrous ideas are dancing through your mind and you can't wait to share them with your reader. So, while you're in this state of peak enthusiasm, you can't hold back and you decide to jump right into the writing phase of your book.

Don't do it!

You may get off to an amazing start. But soon the ideas start to run dry and you come up short on content. That's when a detailed outline you can refer to instantaneously is a huge advantage.

If you haven't already plugged in all the details, your writing will grind to a halt. You interrupt the flow and will probably have a more difficult time getting back into the spirit later. The clear direction a completed outline provides saves you the unnecessary anguish. **Once you do get rolling with a completed outline, there's no stopping you.**

Many are successful in launching projects. They have the skill, the ability and the background to write a wonderful book. So they jump right in, feet first. Problem is... they don't adequately prepare themselves in advance.

Of all the thousands of books completed and marketed each year, I'd guess that thousands more were started with equally ambitious intentions. Those would-be authors lunged forward by putting words into sentences... and sentences into paragraphs. But sooner or later, they hit a speed-bump and dropped their engines on the road. They simply didn't know what to write next and their dreams of writing a successful book suddenly came to an abrupt halt.

I know it's tempting to just want to get on with it. You've got the knowledge inside and you're eager to share it. But you must resist the temptation. I urge you to create a detailed plan first and then and only then should you write your masterpiece.

Without a complete plan you'll wander off course. It's very easy to do as you get caught up in the creative process. Equipped with an outline, you have the framework of your book right beside you. So staying on track is much easier.

Perhaps the most useful advantage of completing a detailed outline as a preliminary step is the continuity it brings. Once you start writing... there's nothing to impede your progress... nothing to get in your way.

You can go until you decide it's time for a break. You won't have to stop midstream and ponder your next point and you can pick it up at any time and get back into the flow of "writing mode" much more easily.

It's all there in black and white, so you can simply pick it up at any time and instantly, you're right back in the writing groove. It's much easier to get it done when you do your thinking ahead of time. You'll have to proceed and write your book using this concept to fully grasp and appreciate what a wondrous gift a detailed outline really is.

I'll share the complete step-by-step details of creating a magical outline a little later. For now just try to appreciate the fact that your completed plan is like a chunk of ore that's loaded with gold. All you have to do is process it by turning raw information into complete sentences and paragraphs. That's when the true value becomes apparent to everyone... even though it's essentially in your hands at the completed outline stage.

Seeing a Mountain... Instead of a Valley

Perspective is everything. Writing a full-size book can be a little intimidating – particularly your first time around. It's a full-size project to be sure. But with a little support and guidance, you will get your book written and in far less time than most people think is possible for an accomplished writer.

It's important to trust yourself. If you weren't capable of writing your book, you never would have had the dream in the first place.

Focus on the result... not the challenge you may encounter at any time during the creation process. Keep your eye on the prize – having your completed book before you – instead of thinking about how much you still have to do. Keep the end in mind and your enthusiasm will sustain you.

Make full use of the proven shortcuts you're about to discover and what seems like a monumental task will be nothing more than a routine project. Have faith in yourself and in the process. It works -- every time.

Not Making a Habit of Success

Maximum productivity means taking positive steps every day. Regular action towards your goal without relenting ensures that you reach it. Make daily progress. Do something every day that advances you towards the successful completion of your book.

Stay focused and committed to your project. Keep it in the forefront of your mind. You've made it your priority, now stick with it.

If you look at it as one major project consisting of hundreds of pages, it's easy to get swallowed-up and become overwhelmed by the magnitude of a book-writing project. When you put it off for even a few days, it's more difficult to regain your rhythm. But picking up the pieces and continuing along is effortless when you're constantly thinking about it.

Consider each chapter a major component and each subsection as one essential piece of the complete puzzle.

Write one section at a time. Then move on to another. With each individual segment, you're another step closer to realizing your objective.

It's this kind of bite-size writing that makes the seemingly overwhelming task of crafting 100 to 200 pages far easier. Breaking it down is a major key to accomplishment. "By the yard it's hard... but by the inch, it's a cinch" is a truism that's particularly relevant to book writing.

Not Taking Care of the Important Things

Your book must be high on your to-do list in order for you to take the necessary steps to see it through. But you can only be 100% effective on your book project when you ensure that other important things in your life aren't forgotten.

This may seem obvious to you, but getting so wrapped up in your writing and becoming oblivious to the world around you can happen to anyone and the consequences can all but wipe out any forward progress you've achieved with your undivided attention.

Peace of mind is a fundamental requirement for successful writing. Sure, you need a quiet spot to let your fingers glide magically across the keyboard, but without peace of mind, you'll be unable to sustain your concentration for any length of time.

Be sure to take care of the important things like spending quality time with family, monitoring what your kids are doing, paying the bills, and keeping food on the table. To get your book finished, you'll want to minimize the worries, upsets and concerns. Putting out fires constantly can drain anyone. A conflict-free household is important and helps you move smoothly towards accomplishment.

The world doesn't stop when you're busy writing. Keep this in mind and you'll find your time alone to be much more pleasurable, productive, and profitable.

Not Establishing Your Own Personal Sanctuary

As a writer there are few tools you must have. But a quiet place to work is crucial, particularly at the beginning of your project. You need peace and quiet to concentrate and organize your thoughts and to craft these concepts into a finished product.

Find a place where you can work uninterrupted. Consider a corner in the basement or any free room you happen to have. If you've already got an office set up at home –perfect! Your private sanctuary awaits you.

Essentially what you want to establish is a place of productivity. Free of television, radio, computer games, emails, and chatter – your sanctuary is your personal space where your book takes shape.

Finding a place at home is ideal, as the close proximity makes it easy to get work done at regular intervals. But if you don't have a place where you can concentrate at home, or like me, you thrive in different environments, take your book writing on the road. A favorite approach of mine is to take my laptop and visit a local park. Working from the car, or even a quiet corner at Starbucks can often lead to a productive hour-long writing session.

When you can free your mind and focus entirely on the project at hand, you'll make a noticeable leap in your productivity.

Creative expression thrives in a peaceful environment. That's not to say you can't write segments amidst noise and chaos. But if you have to write your entire book this way, you're making it way more difficult on yourself than it need be.

Allowing Molehills to Become Mountains

Like any project in any category, business, or situation in life, unexpected challenges come up. It's only natural. Even with the most thorough, detailed planning, you'll probably still encounter the occasional roadblock. Recognize it and move on.

Don't let the little things get in your way. If you're missing a key quote, or an important idea just isn't coming to you, simply move on to the next segment. You'll spend more time and disrupt an otherwise productive session when you get away from writing. Simply take note of the missing piece and get back in the flow. Don't stop to examine the hurdle or you may not even finish the race.

Handle obstacles one at a time.
When faced with problems or challenges as you write your book, simply ponder these two questions...

  1. **What does this problem mean?**
  2. **What should I do about it?**

Minor challenges can quickly become overwhelming problems that can threaten your entire book project. The best advice is to keep moving forward. "Through adversity to the stars" as my Dad is fond of saying. Remember, it's not what happens to you that matters most – it's what you do about it. That is what makes the difference.

Problems test your resolve. Don't let them infringe on your advances.

Make a note of each problem and deal with it at the appropriate time. Once you're into writing mode and the words are flowing like magic – don't stop for anything. Any obstacle should be noted and then set aside until the bulk of your writing is complete. You can always go back after your draft is complete and fill any holes.

Finding Excuses

It's human nature to want to take the easy route. Staring at a blank page, hundreds of pages away from completion, your natural reaction might be to create diversion. Perhaps writing a complete book is just too difficult a task – at least it can seem that way in these moments of uncertainty, frustration and despair.

Don't let it stop you! Many fall into this trap... and that's precisely the reason why most people never write a book.

Hey, it's easy to find excuses. Think long and hard about it and you might even find an excuse that a "no excuses" teacher might find acceptable for a late assignment. But who are your really fooling? What's more... if you don't follow through and get your book finished, you're actually doing a disservice to all those people who could benefit big-time from all your interesting and high-value information.

Demand more of yourself. Do it just once – right here, right now.

Get your book written in the next 30 days and it will transform you as an individual. You'll amaze yourself with your creativity, skills and perseverance. Never again will your be stopped by the potholes along the way.

Biting Off More Than You Can Chew

Choose too broad a topic and you'll only frustrate yourself. Don't write the definitive guide to all forms of advertising – start with postcards, classified ads, or direct mail inserts – if that's something you've already mastered.

Don't write about every species of bird found in North America -- stick to those that frequent your summer home in cottage country.

If your subject area is too general in scope, you can't do an adequate job of covering it in 200 pages or less. Breaking it down gives your book a target audience and makes it much more useful to the reader.

Writing about something you don't know well is another recipe for disaster. Start with what you know, or are passionately interested in learning about. Do your research before putting pen to paper. Don't short-cut this vital step. You need to have a rock-solid resource from which to draw upon. If you're trying to wing it, you'll only get so far. Even if you bluffed you way through an entire book, your product would fall flat on its face as you'd be doing the reader more harm than good.

If you don't know – don't write. Uncover the best information and cast it in your own words using your own examples, insights and experience.

Avoid writing about anything that isn't interesting to you. If it's a challenge to write due to a lack of interest on your part -- imagine what it's like to read!

The solution is to regroup. Narrow your focus. Zoom in on any area of specialty and interest.

Refine your thesis to make it more specific and to the point. Redirect your efforts to produce a book of from 100 to 200 pages. Forget writing a 700-page monster. If you've got that much information to share, make it three books instead of one. But do get your first book written at all costs.

Chapter Four: A Business Mindset Means More Sales & Profits For You

Serve Your Market

Fundamental business principle number one is to give the buyer exactly what she wants. When you deliver what the market already desires – more customers will naturally find your book because it addresses the issue on their minds.

Find a problem in need of a solution. Discover a method to enhance the quality of life in a significant way for your target market. Then shape your book to suit. Starting from the potential buyer's perspective helps you create a product they'll want to scoop up -- as soon as it's available.

Marketplace "wants" may be more obvious if your niche is something you know well. If for example, you write about your profession, you may already be in touch with a widespread desire that's just aching to be filled.

Help buyers play the role they want to play.

Ideally, your book should shortcut the process, making it easier to get results fast. Provide key answers, solutions, helpful advice, tips, techniques, time-saving methods, inside secrets, and so on. Give them what they need to get to where they want to go – in the shortest timeframe possible.

Your book should fill a void. I'm writing this particular text to give you the answers I wish I had before attempting my first book. Supply the missing link and you'll find a built-in market for your work. The closer the connection between the "wants" of prospective buyers and the solutions you provide, the greater your likelihood of success.

Get to know your market. Discover what it is they really want to know to help solve or problem or advance them closer to a goal. Then give them exactly what they want.

Make It Easy

Supply specific "hands on" information – something your buyer can use and benefit from right away. It's important that you relate to the reader on their terms. This means coming from a position of understanding... where you can put yourself in your buyer's shoes and see things through their eyes.

Give buyers everything they could possibly need to attain the desired result. Make your information easy to read and even easier to apply. Don't leave out any vital information. But don't bog them don't with unnecessary filler either. Respect your customers and their time.

Break it down into small tasks that are doable. Shorten the path by supplying action steps buyers can take today, to get to their point of payoff that much sooner.

Help buyers get the most out of tools they already have... and give them additional tools and support materials to aid them further.

Provide solid, helpful information that's well organized. Give your readers a jump start with a table of contents, descriptive chapter topics, and perhaps a key point summary.

Don't make your book an academic volume that needs to be studied to be appreciated. Fast, pertinent information of value and specific relevance is what today's non-fiction book buyer is looking for. Quick and easy solutions that work, supplied in simple, everyday English is a formula that works every time.

Give More Value

Think about how some of the top businesses operate. The best restaurants for example, provide every convenience and comfort to their customers -- from valet parking to superb gourmet meals and a vast selection of fine wines from their own cellar.

No detail is overlooked. They know what customers want and they deliver it down to the finest detail. That's exactly how you should treat your book buyers too.

Offer more of the most relevant information. Over deliver on key content – that's what the best non-fiction books do. They're jammed with solid information, insights and resources... and they're short on filler.

Any book you write should promise much and deliver even more. Don't hold anything back. Uncover every nugget -- and then some. Give it everything you've got so your buyer feels absolutely delighted with their purchase.

Strive to give buyers at least ten times more in "use value" than you ask from them in "cash value".

 Remember, it's the information contained between the covers of your book that your buyer wants. So it really only costs you a little more in terms of effort to deliver extra quality material your customers can understand and apply. Do that and they'll appreciate you, help spread the word about your book and come back for more should you release additional, related titles down the road.

Provide Superb Customer Service

Make it easy for prospects, customers and the media to get in touch with you. Accessibility is one key to providing great service. Email works great as a non-intrusive medium for self-published writers. Just be sure to check your mail often and respond promptly and professionally.

Explain all the critical details and outline the most important points up-front and you simplify the buying decision for prospects. Give them the relevant information they need to make an informed decision in the moment.

The more you tell, the more you sell. Describe your product thoroughly in your sales copy. Address every conceivable question, or make yourself available to address any concerns people may have about you or your book. Given the choice, it's best to provide the answers up front in any sales copy and on your website.

Today's buyer expects and deserves prompt service. Don't take 5 days to answer email, as an electronics manufacturer recently did with my inquiry. That's just bad business.

As with any other enterprise, as a self-published author, you're in the business of serving customers. Answer all inquiries the same day they're received and personalize your messages. Show people that you're genuine and that you really do care about them. Simple business etiquette can only lead to additional book sales which puts more money in your pocket.

Be expedient in your service. If you're receiving hard-copy orders for your book, ship them out immediately. Buyers like it when you rush their shipments and place a high priority on delivering what they want as quickly as possible.

Whenever there's a delay (whether your fault, or not) you can count on hearing about it from your customer. But you can keep problems down to an absolute minimum by carefully packaging and promptly shipping out packages as orders are received. If you're selling your book via digital delivery methods, keep on top of it to make sure all systems are "go" and everything (order buttons, download pages, payment processors, etc.) are all functioning as they should.

Create a pleasant experience for the buyer. Act on their behalf. Show heartfelt gratitude and concern for their utmost satisfaction. Leave your prospect or customer with nothing but good feelings and you'll sell more books through word of mouth.

Marketing is Key

Marketing is an essential component to reaping the greatest rewards from your writing endeavors. As an author/self-publisher/entrepreneur... you're also the marketing director of YOU Inc. This means that responsibility for the success or failure of your venture rests squarely on your shoulders.

As a self-published author, book sales are your primary source of revenue. The more copies you sell, the more cash flows in and the greater your net profits after expenses are paid. Just as customers are the lifeblood of every business, buyers are vital to your successful book venture.

Effective marketing brings buyers to you. Any actions you take – directly or indirectly – to win over book buyers would be considered "marketing" in one way or another. Your sales letter, press release, promotional postcard, directory listing, question and answer sheet, blog, website and others are marketing tools you may or may not employ. So too is your book's title, cover and table of contents.

Each contact with a prospect or customer is in effect, marketing. It could be face-to-face, over the telephone, via email, or while the prospect or customer visits your site. But each encounter leaves an impression – positive or negative – and so each point of contact is essentially a marketing opportunity.

Marketing isn't a one-time thing – it's an ongoing process that begins while your book is still at the idea stage. It's about spotting a hungry market and supplying exactly what that market wants.

Effective marketing begins by creating a title that captures attention and arouses interest, while leading prospects towards making a purchase.

Consistency helps keep your book alive and selling well for years. In his book, 1001 Ways To Market Your Book, John Kremer suggests doing 5 things each day in the area of marketing. This is sound advice. Taking daily marketing action is the best way to ensure a steady stream of book sales over the long haul.

As author, you're also the chief spokesperson, promoter, and sales manager for your book. Success or failure is in your hands. Your outcome is largely up to you.

Your product either makes you money month after month, or it falls flat on its face and fizzles out quickly. But make no mistake – few businesses succeed long term without an effective and consistent marketing action plan.

Set Your Targets and Reach Them

Most successful businesses set sales objectives regularly. They prepare forecasts as part of their regular business planning. You should too.

76

Setting a target gives you something concrete and tangible to shoot for. You're not just hoping for the best... and praying that you'll get there.

In the beginning, choosing an appropriate target can be challenging, since you don't have past experience to draw from. Past performance is a major component of sales forecasting for most businesses. But don't let this stifle you. Set a goal that forces you to reach high... but not one that requires the perfect alignment of the planets and the luck of a lottery jackpot winner to pull off.

Leo Hauser said it best when he suggested we aim higher. "Shoot for the moon. Shoot for the moon because even if you miss, you'll still end up among the stars. But what do most people do? They shoot for the barn door. Then when they miss it... what do you think they land in? It ain't stardust, I can tell you that."

Establish your target, then figure out how you're going to get there. Consider all possibilities such as free publicity, joint ventures with other publishers or entrepreneurs, special offers to your industry, interest groups, associations or communities, advertising, bulk sales, even selling on Amazon and eBay. Multiple sales channels mean multiple sources of revenue – something every successful business seeks.

Deadlines Are Your Best Friend

Without deadlines, how much work would actually get done? Truth is... deadlines enhance productivity. As time ticks away, the pressure increases to just get the job done – whatever it takes.

Deadlines can be a terrific ally at various stages of your book venture. When your back is against the wall and there's no alternative but to roll up your sleeves and get down to business, something wonderful happens. It's remarkable just how productive one becomes when there's no other way out.

Used effectively, deadlines force you to take a business-like approach to writing and marketing your book. Set a time limit for your writing. Establish an actual date in the not too distant future when your book will be completed. Make it 30 days or less from today. Commit to it. Know that you've got to get serious if you want to make serious money.

Once your draft is complete, set a new deadline a few days later for turning your rough manuscript into a polished piece complete with an attractive layout and front and back covers. Next, set another deadline for the creation of your marketing materials -- and then another to implement your marketing plan.

Stick to it and knock off one objective at a time. Get away from any "comfort-zone" thinking. Challenge yourself. Respect every deadline. Commit to meeting each one... and reach it you will. You might even surprise yourself in the process.

Understand Why People Will Buy Your Book

Like any successful business, the author/self-publisher needs to know what makes the market tick. What does your prospective buyer really need and want that your book provides? It's crucial to identify this before your book takes shape. But it's also very important to stress the underlying desires of your prospect in every marketing effort.

People want their:

Problems to be solved...
Burdens to be lifted...

Symptoms to be alleviated...
Hurts need to be healed...
Unhealthy conditions need to be reversed...

And they want to...

Learn new skills...
Discover ways to get more out of life...
Expand their existing knowledge...

At the root of every successful non-fiction book is an underlying current condition – a condition the buyer wants to change. Help lift your reader from where she is in the moment to where she'd really like to be and you've got a certain formula for success.

It's human nature to want more. It's this driving force that leads to new developments, inventions, and books that make attaining the desirable – faster and easier than anything currently available. Fulfill the deep desires of your target reader and you'll have a winning book that could earn you a whole lot of money.

Help the reader acquire new skills and abilities. Organize your information so she can step right into a role... and perform like a master. It's the quick realization of desires – instant gratification -- that today's book buyer wants.

Crash courses that propel them up the knowledge ladder in the fewest hours are in hot demand. An example might be a book on woodturning that teaches readers to turn raw woods into beautiful bowls without the usual years of training. Simply supply what the market wants and help them attain the results they desire quickly and as easily as possible. It's this road many successful businesses take and it's the one I urge you to follow too.

Little Things Make a Big Difference

Your book is your product. It's the physical representation of you and your enterprise. Take the time to make it a quality creation – one that not only contains valuable information but one that presents the information in a way that's easy for readers to grasp and implement.

Basic editing is a must. Do your best to correct any obvious spelling mistakes. Eliminate run-on sentences. Remove excessive words. Keep an eye out for overused words, phrases and well-worn clichés. Ensure that each paragraph flows smoothly into the next. Clean up your text by making it a more readable and informative presentation on the topic.

Glaring errors interrupt and annoy readers as they try to process information. So do your best to make your work as professional as possible. You might not catch everything (apologies to all my readers because I never get it quite right myself) but you will make tremendous improvements by reviewing and editing your manuscript prior to its release.

Review what you've written at least once before publishing. If you can get others to check over your material and make note of any typos, spelling mistakes, and obvious inconsistencies –that's even better.

Don't Undervalue Your Product

First time authors have a tendency to undervalue their work. It may be difficult for you to fathom anyone spending more than a few dollars for your book. But I can assure you, the right book directed at a targeted audience can often fetch a whole lot more. In some venues, lower prices thrive and an effective strategy there requires volume. But selling your book via online or offline direct marketing methods often means you can sell your product at double or triple typical bookstore prices.

That's another overwhelming advantage of non-fiction vs. fiction: you can charge considerably more money for highly specialized and targeted, niche market information.

Avoid mass-market thinking. As a self-publisher, you're not in direct competition with bookstore titles that are printed in quantities of several thousand copies each time. Few in your target group of prospective buyers will choose another title over yours, just to save a few dollars on the cover price. Success in bookselling is about creating irresistibility. You can charge a premium – even as a first time author – simply by creating a piece of work your specific readers can't wait to get their hands on because it provides something no other resource does.

Realistically, it's highly unlikely an entrepreneur marketing from his or her own website can make enough of a profit at $10 per sale to stay in business very long. Even slashing your costs to the bare bone with electronic delivery methods isn't enough. If you're relying on your own marketing efforts, you would likely have to sell an enormous number of books and have a more profitable back-end product to make such a scenario viable economically.

You can still sell low cost information by hooking up with a publishing platform and tapping into the new and growing e-reader craze. To succeed on a larger scale, you'll likely need to write multiple books.

But don't worry about that. In many cases, your potential customer will gladly pay for your inside secrets. So don't be afraid to charge higher than usual prices if you offer valuable information. Buyers are still getting your genuine expertise for pennies on the dollar of what experts, consultants, and other specialists typically charge for their time. A higher price can often get you into profitability much faster.

Think Long Term

Take your book writing and publishing venture seriously. Avoid being a "flash in the pan" or a "one-hit wonder". There's really no point in making a splash, if you're only going to fade fast. Plan to stick around for the long haul. This kind of long distance view forces you to take a more businesslike approach to decisions you make and the actions you take.

Always be on the lookout for ways to increase your sales and profits. Add sales through volume discounts. Consider selling to distributors, stores, online merchants, catalogues, libraries and government training programs. You might also position your book as a gift item by offering a gift wrapping option to buyers.

Do take advantage of special days on the calendar. If you've written 101 Ways For Hopeless Men to Quickly Rekindle The Romance, it's ideally suited to Valentine's Day, so gaining free media exposure and reaping the profits of this additional attention is much easier.

As you drive towards the finish line of your book, begin to entertain the possibility of follow-up titles. That's where you can earn some serious money.

Imagine having 4 or 5 separate books related to your subject area. At first glance it may seem like a stretch – particularly for the "non-writer". But it's a proven strategy to multiplying your profits exponentially. You simply dovetail your first product into the second, creating a link between two different books. You can then add several more titles the same way.

From a business point of view, this concept is brilliant. Author of The Mega Strategy, Dan Lee Dimke, suggests creating numerous follow-on titles. He has personally sold millions of self-published books and tapes using this exact concept, what he terms the "Concatenation Principle".

Essentially it means pre-designing each book and promotional package used to sell it, so the two together simultaneously create a genuine desire in the mind of the reader to acquire the next book in the series.

It's not only a logical decision... but an emotional one as well. Logically, it makes sense to get the next edition and add to the reader's knowledge bank. Emotionally, the buyer wants the whole enchilada and doesn't want to risk missing out on any crucial secret. After being blown away by the information in your first book, the buyer is driven by a compelling desire for more – and the only way to quench this desire is to buy your next book.

The most challenging and costly sale is the sale to the first-time customer.

Think about it. The first-timer doesn't know you or your material. So you've got to get the word out – which often means advertising – and good advertising venues have a cost attached.

But over-deliver great information and top-drawer value and you'll sell readers again and again by simply bringing your newest book to their attention. Create a natural link to your latest product and you'll find lots of previous buyers are delighted to snap up your latest offering too.

Creating a related series of books isn't the only way to establish additional revenue for your business. An early edition of The Sales Bible by Jeffrey Gitomer had audio CD's attached, adding perceived value to the product and boosting the price for the publisher.

Many books inspire calendars or reference guides featuring the same theme. Jeffrey Lant, author of How To Make A Whole Lot More Than $1,000,000 Writing, Commissioning, Publishing and Selling "How To" Information creates numerous reports from each book he writes, thus providing multiple choices for buyers... additional lower-cost options... and extra income sources for his publishing business.

Chicken Soup For The Soul quickly turned into multiple entries targeting specific niches with titles like Chicken Soup For the Teacher's Soul... Chicken Soup For The Kid's Soul... Chicken Soup For The Horse Lover's Soul... and even Chicken Soup For The Prisoner's Soul. Talk about cashing in on a profitable theme!

Create additional opportunities for buyers of your book to get even more. Do this and you'll increase the value of the average purchase – a major factor in improving the profits of your venture.

Think Globally

In case you hadn't noticed, the world has become a smaller place. International markets, once the exclusive domain of large corporations with fat bank accounts, are now easily accessible to practically anyone with a home computer.

Most books can be shaped to reach far beyond the limits of local, regional, or even national appeal. Many skills, techniques, concepts and tactics have universal applications. Unless your topic is specific to one particular area such *as* The Northwest Herb Lover's Handbook -- consider a wider geographical area your sales could span. But if your topic is something like Turning Wood Scraps Into Functional Furniture... or Making Gifts They'll Adore Every Time... you can potentially sell your book all over the world.

84

I'm going to assume that your book will be written in English. According to David Crystal, author of The Cambridge Encyclopedia of the English Language, one out of four of the world's population speaks English to some level of competence. English is the main language of books, newspapers, airports, air-traffic control, international business, academic conferences, science, technology, diplomacy, sport, international competitions, music and advertising. No other language has as much international acceptance and applicability. But it's clearly not the only language of book buyers.

Don't be surprised to receive orders from people who understand English but who happen to reside in predominantly non-English speaking countries. There's another potential profit center – the marketing of foreign language rights to your work. (For more information in selling foreign book rights, you might want to see Paulette Ensign's course at tipsbooklets.com among others)

Write your book and sales material in an easy, conversational style so anyone can read and understand your message without struggling.

This is particularly important for those whose first language is something other than English. Simply facilitate and welcome all orders and you could be pleasantly surprised by the markets you reach.

Conserve Resources

However small your beginnings, if you want to generate an attractive income from book writing, it's crucial that you operate as a business. Keep costs to a minimum.

It's easy to let incidental expenses like office or shipping supplies get way out of hand. Buy only what you need and shop for reasonable prices. You don't have to become a penny-pinching fanatic, but paying attention to every outgoing dollar gets you to profitability sooner... and helps keep you there.

Only print the hard-copy books you know you can sell within the next two to three weeks. Take advantage of "Just-In-Time" delivery of supplies and "Print-On-Demand" publishing. There's no bigger mistake you could make as a self-publisher than to tie up your cash flow in inventory. I know you believe in your book. That's a good thing. But don't commit large amounts of money unnecessarily. In business, cash really is king. It's a precious resource – particularly for the fledgling business – so don't squander it.

Conserve cash wherever you can. Spend intelligently. If you don't, you'll invariably regret it. Avoid obvious expenses your newborn business doesn't need like special equipment and software beyond the basics to create and layout your book and cover design.

Avoid paying for things such as photography, elaborate cover creations, fancy artwork and other graphics services – at least when you're getting started. You can always hire that kind of expertise later after you've made a bunch of money. These things are only secondary contributors to sales, at best.

Market wisely. There's no greater return on investment than that paid by free media exposure in a venue that reaches your precise target audience.

For the price of an envelope and postage stamp – or time spent online investigating ideal targets – you could potentially generate thousands of dollars in instant sales from a single press release. You could even send releases by fax or email if you wanted to, as long as it's done in the right way. This will save a little cash on postage costs and get your "news" at the intended destination that much sooner.

The opposite of a great return on investment is to waste you money buying prospect lists from shady dealers. Purchase anything like the "names and email addresses of one million prospects and buyers" and you might as well burn hundred dollar bills in the fireplace. These types of offers should be avoided at all costs. It's not just the money you'll spend... but the irreparable damage you'll create by "spamming" others.

A far better marketing option is to use lead-generation advertising and invite prospective book buyers to contact you, or visit your web site for more information. Anyone who raises their hand to show interest, or actively seeks out more information on your books is a genuine, highly-qualified prospect. This is the type of individual who is far more likely to buy the book you have to offer.

Chapter Five: 6 Simple Guidelines To Sure-Fire Writing Success

Think it Through In Advance

Think before you write. Before putting pen to paper or fingers to the keyboard – prepare your piece. It only takes a few minutes to map out the ideas for each section of your book. But doing so gives you the guidelines to take you in the direction you intend.

Writing is fun and surprisingly easy. Never in my wildest dreams would I have ever envisioned myself uttering such a sentiment - until a few short years ago. That's when I discovered the magic of a well thought-out plan as a prerequisite to easy writing. Fact is... when you know what you're going to say, writing is a breeze. It's as easy as opening your mouth and moving your lips to speak about something you want to say.

You wouldn't travel by car across the country without a map – unless, perhaps you lived in tiny Luxembourg. A basic map would point you in the right direction, but that's about it. Yet a detailed map would lead you from street by street, mile after mile to your ultimate destination.

That's exactly what your book outline or plan does. It makes for a much more efficient and hassle-free journey. You simply chart your course, one step at a time until you reach your target. The end result is never in question because you have a definite purpose and all the help you need to get there.

But try writing without a plan and at some point you'll hit a wall. Without an outline, it's difficult to get going, although once inspired the words tend to flow for the time being. But you're writing a book here, not an office memo.

You might be able to crank out plenty of words when you're feeling up to it, but are those words as direct, purposeful and helpful to the reader as they could be?

Without a solid outline, ultimately you'll find yourself staring at a blank page with nowhere to go. Why put yourself through such agony? It reminds me of those terribly frustrating moments writing essay-based exams and feeling the pressure of coming up dry as time was quickly running out.

Map Out an Outline in Easy Steps

An outline helps you funnel your information and present it in the most powerful, effective and usable way.

Outlining allows you to shape your idea by taking a broad concept and channeling it in a specific direction. This is what gives your book an original angle. It's your personal stamp on your product. You simply move from the more general information about your topic to the specific details.

If you were writing about how to keep your kids fit and active in an era where video games rule, you might list activities like bicycling, rollerblading, skateboarding, skating and swimming as major chapters. Each activity could then be explored in greater detail. The chapter on bicycling could include such subtopics as: riding safety, rules of the road, creating opportunities for riding, how to make riding a favorite activity, etc.

Outlining forces you to establish a framework. Having a completed outline before you write is like having a detailed blueprint before you build. It makes the task of writing a book far more fun and easy.

Outlining forces you to think things through in the beginning. This is important as once you get on a roll and the words start to flow like magic, you won't have to stop to think about what you're going to say next. You simply progress through your plan and take the key points you've entered in your outline and compose those into sentences fast and furiously.

A detailed outline means your book is as good as written. It's money in the bank to you. Always prepare an outline and your book will fall into place with greater ease and in less time than you ever imagined.

Mind Mapping Makes Outlining Easy

I encourage you to use mind mapping as the first step in developing your book idea and creating your outline. Mind Mapping is an excellent way to generate and connect ideas with other ideas.

With mind mapping, you place the core concept in words, images, or both in the center of the page. Nest, you "free associate" – listing everything related to your main topic as it comes to you. Then you connect those words to your central idea with lines radiating from the core concept in the middle of the page.

Mind mapping can be an intense creative exercise. You focus on the big idea and then you quickly produce associated words, ideas and examples. The main thing is to write everything down in key word concepts. Capture your creativity without judging – there will be plenty of time later to assess each idea and determine if it fits with the theme of your book.

Mapping is a simple yet highly-effective method to unshackle your mind so you can think without restraint in a non-linear way. Once you get used to the process of mind mapping, you'll want to use it for each section of your book and you'll quickly generate more ideas than you can actually use. This is ideal because it enables you to select only the best information for inclusion.

Since you're in the idea-generation mode while mapping, there's no editing or evaluating involved. It's only about ideas and associations. Not all your captured details will be useful – but that's okay.

Keep generating ideas and you'll continue to engage your natural creativity. The more ideas you produce, the more you'll have to pick from. Ultimately, you end up with a collection of key elements that are a good fit for your book.

Creating a mind map is like thinking on paper. Once done, you're on your way to completing your book fast.

You already have some useful knowledge and experience that can help thousands. But it serves no useful purpose until you shape it into a useable product and make it available to others.

Most stop short of completing their book because they grow weary of the process. But in minutes, you'll see your book concept come to life with mind mapping and this information can then be transformed into a clear and workable outline.

Anyone can find a market with a problem, gather data and outline a project within hours if you already know the subject matter, or a few days if research is required. Then it's just a matter of organizing your information into an outline and writing your book.

Gather Information

Collecting pertinent information is another preliminary step that needs to be taken. The total book planning process might involve collecting data, searching specific information, interviewing experts and organizing bits of information into a format that makes sense. Gather as much key information as you can before shaping it into your book.

Once you've narrowed down a topic and you're sure it's a winner, stick with it. Focus your efforts like a laser beam. Be open to new information as you uncover it. But don't get sidetracked by going off on a tangent that's far removed from your overall concept. The more your focus on your topic, the more information you'll find that relates to it. Much of it is usable material that can make your book better.

Tap into rich resources at your disposal. Librarians are very helpful in locating specific information. Be sure to let them know you're working on a book and most will be delighted to help you locate the information you seek.

Consider your own personal library of books, CD's, home-study courses, magazines and trade journals and all those ebooks on your computer or e-reader.

Look inside your filing cabinet too if you've been clipping articles for years. You may already have a stack of background material from which to get ideas and add perspective and unique flavor.

Make full use of the multitude of valuable online resources – rich sources of quality information that's right at your fingertips.

Check Your Sources

Insist upon providing only accurate information. Don't just accept what you read or hear... and don't automatically reject it either. Acknowledge the information and check it out, as any good journalist would.

Conduct your own investigations. Track down the author, speaker, or quoted expert. Confirm the information and dig for more. This verifies your earlier findings and gives you additional material straight from the horse's mouth.

Your best bet is start from a solid foundation of understanding. That's why writing about your profession, trade or favorite activity makes it so easy. You've already accumulated a ton of knowledge.

With an inside understanding, chances are much of what you do is automatic. Now it's a reflex action based on habit. You've got it down so effectively that you don't have to think about it.

You probably know a lot more than you think. The trick is to identify and articulate the things you tend to take for granted. These are the hidden secrets your reader hasn't been privy to... but definitely wants to know.

Speaking as an informed expert gives you the confidence to openly share. You don't have to second guess anything – you know how it works better than anyone else. Simply take this foundation of knowledge and translate it in your own way to make it interesting, informative and more helpful than anything else on the market.

Details Make the Difference

Anyone can rough out an outline in a matter of minutes. All it takes is a topic subject and at least seven major subjects relating to your topic.

Let's say you're an advertising copywriter and you want to write a book about sales letters. Here's an example of what your rough outline might look like...

Introduction
Keys to Successful Sales Letters
Why People Buy – Understanding Buyer Psychology
Putting Emotion into Your Message
The Sales Letter Plan
Winning Formulas for Profitable Sales Letters
Headlines That Command Attention
Openings That Draw Prospects Inside
Deliver Benefits That Appeal
Back Up Your Claims with Proof
Creating Irresistible Offers
Add a Strong Guarantee
Go For the Close
Add a Postscript for Extra Power
Create an Order Form That Completes the Sale
Conclusion

This was essentially the basic framework I used for my book on sales letters. What you want to do at this point is identify the major aspects of your book topic. These main elements become chapter topics.

Typically, most nonfiction titles have anywhere from 7 to 30 chapters. If you like to work with easy numbers, shoot for 10 chapters. Write just 10 pages about each chapter topic and you've created a 100-page book.

The next step is to turn your rough outline into a multiple page, detailed book blueprint. Keep your original outline in front of you as you do this as it will help you stay on course.

Take one chapter at a time and fill in the details. Simply answer the questions your reader would have about the chapter topic. That's a great technique and you can often find lots of questions people are asking by searching online forums related to your market niche or general topic.

Using the above example, let's see how we can easily create a detailed chapter plan...

Openings That Draw Prospects Inside

What Makes The Opening So Important?
Why Are Openings So Difficult To Write?
The Best Way to Get Started
Do Salutations Help?
Tried and True Techniques for Creating Riveting Openings
How Opening Paragraphs Encourage Further Reading
How the Headline and Opening Work Together
How Long Should The Opening Be?
The 3 Crucial Tasks Successful Openings Complete
The Quickest Way To Create A Magnetic Opening
Where Most Openings Go Wrong
Examples Of Effective Opening Lines

Your mission is to fill in various bits and pieces about your chapter's subject. Focus on what's most important for your reader to grasp. Keep this thought in mind as you continue to transform a rough shell or skeleton into a detailed outline you can't wait to write.

"What's most important about _____?"

Keep driving towards giving the reader your very best, most beneficial information and guidance.

Anticipate the questions, concerns, obstacles and fears your reader might have. If your book's concept is Gourmet Cooking At Home, one chapter might be titled – Essential Tools For The Home Gourmet.

Now the challenge is to fill in lots of valuable information relating to the chapter idea. Let's assume the role of gourmet chef for a moment, and list some ideas that could work in this chapter.

The #1 Most Important Kitchen Tool You'll Ever Own
Basic Hand Tools Every Home Chef Needs
Helpful Electric Tools To Make Your Job Easier
Versatile Accessories That Save on Dishes
Valuable Time Savers I Learned From the World's Best Chef's
Non-Traditional Kitchen Tools That Open Up Infinite Possibilities
Must-Have Spices and Everyday Ingredients
Establishing an Ideal Work Space
Enhancing Your Favorite Recipes to Create Flavor Explosions
Creating Masterful Culinary Presentations

See how easy it is? There you have 10 ideas created on the fly. You could probably come up with many more for this example. At any rate, a single brainstorming session of just a few minutes was all it took.

The next step in your outline is to settle on those key topics you'll include in the chapter.

If it's a crucial piece of information – you'll want to include it. Depending on the degree of importance and relevance to the chapter's subject, some topics may be reassigned or deleted from the list altogether.

Once you've got it down to the important 7-20 sub-topics, it's time to arrange these. Simply organize the information logically to make it easiest to read and understand. Go from the more general topics to the specific details. Begin at step one and progress sequentially. Organize your information in a way that seems natural to the subject at hand.

Think and Organize – Then Write

To write your book in the shortest time possible requires you to pound away at the keyboard without major interruptions. And nothing forces a more abrupt stop than not knowing what to say next.

But don't you worry – this will never happen to you – if you follow these suggestions.

You now know how to do your thinking ahead of time at the planning stage and map out your book first with an outline, then connect the dots and fill in the blanks.

Evolve your ideas on paper while developing your outline. Don't leave any blank sections to be filled in later. Make it as thorough and complete as you possibly can. If you get stuck, go back to the drawing board and mind map some more.

Establish your concept first. Identify the big idea you want to write about. Find the ideal market for your ideas in book form. Then evolve the concept further with an emphasis on how your book will enhance your reader's life.

Stick with it. Refine your outline as you go based on your research and personal insights. Once you're subject and angle is clearly defined, start to consider the most important ideas you might include as chapter subjects in the book.

As an example, Seeds of Greatness by Denis Waitley consists of 10 chapters. Each chapter deals with one of these key ideas – Self-Esteem, Creativity, Responsibility, Wisdom, Purpose, Communication, Faith, Adaptability, Perseverance, and Perspective.

Let's take a look at a sample chapter called "The Seed of Communication" to see how the author further subdivided this chapter.

Subheadings listed include:

Walking In Another's Moccasins

Getting In On Their Wavelength

Love Letters To Live By

The Sixth Best-Kept Secret of Total Success

Take Time To Listen

Communication Is From Inside To Outside

The Way To Climb Up From "Never"

The Power Of One-On-One

Ten Action Steps To Better Communication

As you can see, this chapter has nine individual sections. This is exactly what you want to do. Chunk it down into chapters. Then with each proposed chapter, break it down even more by creating a list of supporting ideas.

Expand on your book's concept. List the key ideas that describe or define that concept. Then take each of these major ideas and fill in the most significant details. Do this for each chapter and you're off to the races. That's book planning in a nutshell. Breaking it down in this way organizes your thoughts and simplifies the writing process.

Know Your Topic

You're expected to know your subject well. Readers naturally perceive you as an expert in your particular field or topic area. So insist upon a solid foundational understanding before writing a word. If you're dispensing advice and you want to be taken seriously, you better know what you're talking about.

Having a background that qualifies you certainly helps. If you're going to write a guide about how to get a fantastic deal on your next car, knowing how car dealers and manufacturers play the game is essential. Perhaps as a former salesperson, you know the drill and all the techniques used to close the deal at the highest profit. Maybe you worked in management for a dealer and you know the exact latitude dealers have in striking a deal. Maybe you're just passionate about negotiations and you're proud of the phenomenal discounts you've scored in the past.

Each individual background could position you as somewhat of an authority on the subject. It's this level of knowledge and experience – the kind of "inside information" readers don't have – that makes what you have to offer so appealing.

So what if you don't have a background that pre-qualifies you to write about your topic? The best advice I can give you is to just dig in. Study, research, ask questions, and read like there's no tomorrow. If you're passionate about your subject, it will be a labor of love. But if you're not thrilled, genuinely interest and naturally curious, you'll never get it done, like the student who's been assigned a boring topic.

Ask Questions

**"A prudent question is one-half of wisdom." --
Francis Bacon**

Questions trigger answers. It's this quality that makes
questions a valuable tool for completing your book outline at
a record pace.

When someone asks you a question, you naturally feel
compelled to offer a reply. Automatically you enter into
"answer mode" as you quickly formulate a response. We're
wired on autopilot to respond to the trigger. It's as though
you're the next speaker in line and you've just been
introduced. You've got to come up with something... that's
just the way it is. We're conditioned to reply to questions. To
not do so requires more conscious effort than to just go
ahead and submit an answer.

It works the same way when you're exploring the answer to
those questions yourself. Your brain searches its quadrants
and then spits out an answer. Ask the right kind of questions
and you'll find the kind of responses you seek. It's almost
magical once you get used to it.

Two key questions to keep in mind throughout the entire
book writing process are...

1. **What's most important about this?**

2. **How can I help my reader get what s/he wants?**

If you consistently ask yourself these questions, you'll be
unearthing the best information you can provide for your
reader. The more value, insight and authentic assistance you
can provide, the more likely it is you'll succeed.

When launching a new chapter, ponder those 2 questions. Doing so forces you to prioritize information and to focus on the really significant details. To generate key information on each sub-topic, simply ask the golden questions again. The answer will come immediately.

To add more content, ask – who, what, why, where, when and how. Journalists do it – you should too.

Now let's take a look at this idea in practice by creating an example on the fly:

Chapter Topic: How To Build The Perfect Backyard Deck

Possible Subjects:

Design and Layout
City/ Regional Compliance
Hand and Power Tools
Choosing Your Raw Materials
Getting Off To A Good Start
First Things First

Potential Sub-Topic Questions:

Why is it important to establish a precise design and layout before you begin?

Why is it helpful to stake out the area as you work on the design and layout?

What are the most important design elements to consider?

What bylaws are important and relevant for do-it-yourself deck builders?

How do you know if your design is acceptable to everyone who counts?

101

What are the 3 specific steps to follow to prevent a possible problem down the road?

Where can you get power equipment like a post-hole digger and chop saw?

How can you get this entire project completed in a single weekend?

When is the best time of year to build a deck?

How do you select materials so the finished deck looks great and lasts for years?

Where can you find the best deals on deck-building materials and supplies?

See how easy it is? Questions are in fact the answer.

When in doubt, ask a better question. It's a great technique to for creating a detailed outline at hyper-speed.

Break It Down Into Bite Size Pieces

Staring at a blank page when you're shooting for at least 100 pages of text is a little intimidating – particularly when it's your first book. But there's an easy way to overcome this temporary feeling. Simplify the task. Break it down into a series of steps – and then do one step at a time.

If you decided to redecorate your home, you'd probably focus on one room at a time. To tackle it as a single project with ongoing renovations throughout happening simultaneously would be counterproductive and completely inefficient. It would only frustrate you and stifle the best of intentions. What fun is that? Writing IS fun when you chunk it down on focus on one small piece of the puzzle at any given time.

Perspective is everything. See the end result as a project that's coming together nicely as you easily add page after page. If you look at it as a huge, challenging project you doubt you'll ever finish, you're setting yourself up to fail. All you really need to do is focus on the next segment. Get it done – then move on to the next.

Focus on completing an individual section – whether it is 2 short paragraphs or 2 full pages of text. Do this consistently and you'll never get stuck. Anyone can write one segment – it's just one more piece of the puzzle. Just keep your fingers moving. Stay focused on getting your message across. Stick with it for just 5 to 10 minutes and you'll be one segment or one page closer to completion. Put enough of these together and your book is complete.

Get Clear On Your Desired Result

Making the decision to write your book is fine – as long as you stand by it. But not all decisions we make tend to become definitive choices. The word "decide" means to cut off from any other possibility. So let me ask you a question... is your decision to "write your book now" final? Or is it merely a wish you hope to achieve someday? The choice is yours and yours alone.

Since you've read this far I know you're serious about writing a book. Now make your decision to write your book irrevocable. When there's absolutely no turning back, your progress forward accelerates. You've found your wings and nothing is going to stop you now.

Envision the finished product. See your book in your mind's eye and know that's just a matter of _____ (number of written segments) before it's a done deal. The more real the vision, the more likely you are to reach your destination and the sooner you'll get there.

Do whatever it takes. Design your book's front and back cover, or have it designed by a pro. You've made the decision to complete your book, so having the cover professionally designed is merely an investment – one that will pay off.

Next, print the cover and create a mock-up of your book by using a "Clear View" binder (available at any office supply store). Simply insert the cover pages. Add 100 blank pages, or whatever number you're shooting for, and close the cover. There you have it – your book – and it's exactly the way you designed it. Now all you have to do is add some words. Creating a model gives you a clearer vision – making the manifestation much easier.

Get a Great Start

Getting started can be challenging. It can take a segment or two before you find the zone – that blissful state where the words flow effortlessly. It's this stream of consciousness writing that results in quality content that seems to magically appear and it makes writing your book a thrilling adventure.

Just get started. Write something. Loosen up your fingers and kick-start the mind.

Putting pen to paper or fingers to the keyboard is what gets you going. It's like the preliminary warm-up athletes partake in before playing the game.

Don't worry about the words. Just write... and write some more. Never stop to evaluate what you've written. Give yourself permission to write drivel and the pressure ease. Just get it down. Leave any editing until the book is finished.

The more segments you write, the easier it gets.

But how do you launch each segment with a bang? Begin sentences with meaningful, interesting words that pack a punch. Explosive openings create interest and compel the reader to read on. Powerful verbs and descriptive nouns get right to the point making your sentences easier and more interesting to read.

> *If you send me a note, I'll email you my collection of over 1000 "power words" free of charge. Use them whenever you get stuck and you'll find it easier to jump-start those segments and get your writing back into gear - FAST.

Consider key words that best illustrate the most significant aspects of each segment you're writing. These important and descriptive keywords are usually the best choices to launch interesting sentences. Inject vibrancy and action immediately and your words will leap off the page, grab the reader's attention and ensure that she continues reading your book.

Don't Get Hung-Up About Writing

Communication is what writing is all about. It's you communicating your ideas and concepts to a receptive audience. As an author, you hope to express your ideas in the most expedient, direct and colorful way.

"Good writing is good thinking expressed clearly." – Michael Masterson

You've got a point to make – actually numerous points – and you sincerely want to share your information to help your reader. You've got the know-how and the experience. Now it's just a matter of getting it down into a product people can buy.

Think of your writing as nothing more than a meaningful conversation with a friend. You've gathered tremendously valuable information you know your friend will benefit from. Now simply talk to your friend as you would, one-on-one and trust yourself enough to deliver valuable information that genuinely helps your readers.

Forget all pretences of "writing". Dwell on those early experiences as you first attempted to write in school, and you'll only psyche yourself out.

Simply communicate -- convey your information in a way your reader (your friend) will understand, appreciate and accept. In other words... you want to sell your reader on your ideas. Spouting information isn't your goal. Your mission is to genuinely provide valuable assistance to your reader by sharing everything you know about your topic.

Think about one of those deep conversations you've had with a close friend. Maybe it was politics, sports, a major news event, or someone you both know that triggered the discussion. Initially, the exchange might have been nothing more than a casual conversation. But at some point it became much more in-depth, intense and interesting.

With a variation of tones, facial expressions and visual gestures, your communications assumed a more emphatic and dramatic quality. Not only did you hold your own... but you came up with stellar stream-of-consciousness material – quality content that might have even surprised you.

These are precisely the kinds of conversations you want to have with your reader. Throw caution to the wind and let your message get out. Forget that you're even "writing" at all. Consider the writing part of book creation as merely a method for transcribing your thoughts. Just share your best information and get it down on the page.

Create a Productive Environment

Quiet comfort, some basic writing tools and the genuine desire to write your book will make it happen for you.

Free your mind from other distractions during your writing time. Establish an environment that's both comfortable and productive. A separate room with a door works well.

Any kind of computer will save you boatloads of time. A sturdy chair makes it easy to stay focused and adequate lighting minimizes eye strain.

When you close the door behind you, it's time to get down to business.

It's important to let your family know that your "writing time" is sacred. When you enter your environment, it's not to stare at a blank screen daydream, or answer emails. Your mission is to take another step – or several steps towards the finish line of having your book published and on the market.

Give yourself every advantage and let those fingertips flow across the keyboard unimpeded by distraction. You don't need to do this for hours on end. Just commit to doing some writing everyday and your book will be finished soon enough.

With these basics in place, you'll find yourself in good spirits as you begin and delighted with your efficiency in formulating your thoughts into sentences and paragraphs.

Don't Edit Yourself

Proceed with the one task that is before you at any given time and then move on to the next task. Focus is crucial. When you enter into the writing phase of your book, you should do just that – write.

Don't stop to reflect. Don't question what you put down. Don't try to think of an example that might have escaped you. Don't re-write what you've written. In fact, don't edit at all.

Your job is to get your book written in the shortest possible time. You can always fill in the blanks later on, after your initial draft is complete.

Edit as you go and you'll never get it done.

Editing while writing means you'll constantly become frustrated by your slow progress. What's worse is... after you've completed your draft, you'll want to change many details again. Don't do that. Writing is about capturing and expressing ideas as they come to you. Trying to revise, recast or rewrite what you've already put down only interrupts the flow and impedes your progress.

Write whatever comes to mind.

Describe the idea, concept, or technique and efficiently and effectively as you can. Keep going for the duration assigned to that particular segment. If you're writing in 7 minute segments, you've only got 7 minutes to share your best information and the only way you can accomplish this is to keep moving forward. Avoid any evaluation or editing. They'll be plenty of time for that when the writing is done.

Write Each Segment As Fast As You Can

Get it down as quickly as you can and you'll finish your book sooner than you ever thought possible. That's the obvious reason for "speed writing". But there's another benefit of monumental proportions; you'll create excellent material.

When you've got to say it quickly or miss out entirely, you learn to cut to the core message and avoid any non-essentials. The result is work that's direct, to the point, informative and flowing. In short, what you produce is not just information – it's a great read too.

Just remember to write as fast as you can. Keep your fingers busy expressing your thoughts as they emerge. If you can type quickly, you've got a distinct advantage. The faster you can pound out words on to the page, the more you'll accomplish in the same time period.

Get to the good stuff right away – that's what speed writing enables you to do.

With only a matter of minutes to cover each sub-section, you have no choice but to move quickly in order to adequately say what needs to be said. Keep a timer nearby and limit the time you spend writing each small segment to 7 to 10 minutes. At first you might get flustered, but it gets easier as your go along.

Keyboarding 101

If you're not as quick on the keys as you'd like, there are plenty of programs available to help you improve your speed. If you're one of those unfortunate souls like me who never learned basic typing in school, don't despair. It's easier than you think.

Here's a simple method for learning how to type with all your fingers:

Take a fresh page and using the top ¼ of the page or less, type out the exact positioning of all the main keys on your keyboard. Include the top row of numbers and the bottom row that contains the Control, Alt and Space Bar keys. Print the page and cut out the keyboard section and paste or clip it to your monitor.

Next, position your hands so that your fingertips span the middle row of keys.

Leave the G and H key open, separating both hands. Your left hand should have fingers positioned on the A, S, D, and F keys... while the right fingertips are placed on the J, K, L, and colon/semi-colon keys. Force yourself to look that screen instead of the keyboard. When you get stuck, refer to your keyboard printout and touch the appropriate key with the nearest finger.

It may not replace taking a course on basic keyboarding, but it will get you up to speed with the basics in short order. In fact, if you stick with this method, you'll be amazed at your progress in just a few days. Carry on for a couple of weeks and you'll never want to return to two-finger typing again.

Chapter 6: Creating Valuable Content Reader's Will Love

Become an Observer

Pay attention to what's going on around you and you'll tap an ever-abundant source of material. Take it all in at every opportunity.

Often it's the little things that lead to major successes. That's exactly what H. Jackson Brown did and he sold millions of copies of his book – Life's Little Instruction Book. In that book, the author simply shared a collection of wise insights – things your mother or father might have said to you at some point in your young life. This book was written as advice from a father to his son who was heading off to college.

Engage your senses. Keep your eyes and ears open. Notice the things people say, read, do, and complain about. What do they eat, drink, and engage in for entertainment? What draws crowds consistently? How do people like to spend their free time?

What's the biggest complaint you here? Last Christmas, we had the opportunity to spend time with our extended families. As the holidays ended, the recurring complaint heard most often was this: "I have to go back to work on Monday and I'm not looking forward to it one bit!"

It's a shame more people don't find work they enjoy. Instead they slave all week long to earn enough to pay the bills. They might do very well financially... but there's more to life than showing up for work every day just to collect a check. There's got to be plenty of ideas to help people out who find themselves in such a predicament.

Ever wonder why some people always seem happy... or how other folks never seem to age? What secrets do these individuals have up their sleeves? Uncover those gems and you've got some promising book ideas.

Differentiate the key concepts used by successful people. As an example, sales letters written by top marketers and copywriters are available free of charge online. All you have to do start browsing around. These letters provide valuable clues about sales psychology and copywriting tactics and this could a primary source of quality material for a book.

Capture the Moments

Ideas, information and opportunities can present themselves at anytime. Be prepared to capture valuable data, new book ideas, chance encounters, profound words of wisdom, or new sources of material as they become evident to you.

The secret to capturing key moments of opportunity is to always be prepared. Although my wife and I live close to natural green space, I'm seldom prepared with a ready camera when deer, coyotes, foxes and other beautiful creatures of the wild are in clear view from our living room window. These are missed opportunities, usually because I'm deeply involved in other book writing projects.

Keep a pad of paper or notebook with you at all times. Place one in your purse or briefcase, or in the inside pocket of your jacket or daily scheduler/calendar. Keep a small notebook of paper on your night table, one in your car and another on your desk. Don't allow those unexpected golden opportunities to pass you by – seize them in the moment. If you don't document it, there's a good chance you won't remember the idea or important detail when you need to.

Get used to the idea of capturing anything that holds potential value to you for both current and future projects. Cameras and audio recorders are also excellent devices for capturing moments, events and interesting discoveries. The first key is to be prepared. The second key is to label and organize your collected data for easy retrieval. The sooner you get organized, the more likely you are to locate a key detail when you're ready to use it.

Focus on Unique Methods & Perspectives

Focus on creating original material. Putting out something much like that which already exists won't do you or the market any good. Add your own uniqueness, experience and personal touch. Put your stamp on it with a unique twist.

Strive to make your book more helpful and easier to read than the others in your chosen category. Create superior advantages for the prospective buyer. Give them more of exactly the kind of information they want. Deliver more benefits per page than any buyer could ever expect. Fill in the blanks those other products left out.

Capitalize on your individual perspective and experience. Don't be stingy in sharing what you've learned along your life's path.

How has experience changed the way you do things now? That's the kind of valuable material buyers will pay for and it's the kind of detail that is sure to make your book a piece that's clearly distinct from everything else in the market.

Take common industry knowledge and turn it upside down. Show how your methods are more effective. Reveal what you've discovered and demonstrate your results.

Become an Insider

Imagine having inside access to restricted or privileged information. I'm not talking about infiltrating the inner circle of a celebrity only to gossip about it later. What I am referring to is the access you've gained from your unique position in your industry, profession, or association.

Perhaps you've seen the inner workings of companies in your field. For example, you might have learned how one organization demonstrates its environmentally-friendly approach day in and day out. Maybe you recall being employed by a manufacturing firm that had mastered production line techniques, enabling them to cut costs to the bone. You may were trained by an expert tradesman and learned numerous trade secrets and shortcuts to getting the job done the right way in a fraction of the time it would take the average person.

Inside secrets possess tremendous value in the nonfiction marketplace. When shared in book form, they give the reader a crash course in mastery of the subject or task at hand.

Inside information can be uncovered other ways too – though nothing quite compares to the advantages of personal experience. You can often gain access – if not experience – by finding a job in your chosen industry, or by gaining membership to a club or organization. Once inside, think like a journalist. Ask pointed questions, not the vague or rhetorical type, but questions that trigger insightful answers. You're there to gather information so make the most of it whenever you get special access.

Interview Experts

Begin early on to build a list of key experts in your chosen subject area. Add to that list as you discover others with an inside track. It's easiest to get started at the top – those names that are commonly known within a particular field. Add others to the list as their names become familiar to you.

Consider interviewing established and successful experts. Most experts will be happy to answer a few quality questions. The key is to get up to speed on the industry and the expert before you get in touch. Nothing annoys busy people more than those who waste their time by not being prepared. Show that you've done a little research first. You'll be taken much more seriously from the outset.

Don't overlook the crop of fresh new talent emerging on the scene. You'll find lesser known experts more approachable and often very willing to share their views you.

It's a common practice among ebook publishers to send out questionnaires to numerous subject experts asking each to participate and contribute their content to a book project. It's an easy way to compile content and some people have been very successful using this technique. But I'm going to suggest you follow through and write your first book by yourself. You'll feel so much better about it when all is said and done.

As you go about your daily activities, keep be on the lookout for possible interview subjects. Make contacts everywhere you go – trade shows, consumer shows, bookstores, seminars, evening classes, webinars, online forums, training sessions and any kind of special event where your subject specific experts appear.

Ask for business cards or other materials containing contact information and follow-up after the show or event. Get the gig and then do the work composing a few well-developed questions you know readers would love to ask the expert themselves if they were only given the opportunity.

Research Shortcuts

Make full use of the valuable online resources at your disposal. Find out where your potential customers lurk online and get acquainted with the top forums related to your subject. Bookmark these sites and visit them often. Not only will you find many potential customers for your book once it's finished, you'll discover the kind of content people in the market really want. Pay attention and you'll notice recurring questions and concerns. This is one very effective way to uncover what your market wants today.

Visit Google and enter: your market niche + forum. If for example, your book was geared towards online and offline entrepreneurs, you would search Google for "Entrepreneur Forum" or "Small Business Discussion Board" and you'll surely find two of the best forums at warriorforum.com and ablakeforum.com. Here you'll find hundreds of active participants and thousands of lurkers who prefer staying in the background – but who buy related business growth and marketing products with a vengeance as soon as they're unveiled.

Newsletter, ezine and magazine editors are often highly-knowledgeable people who can lead you in the right direction if you'll only take the time to ask politely. Your area librarian is another great contact to make for finding the information you need once you've identified what that information is.

Online resources such as refdesk.com and pearltrees.com can be excellent places to begin your online search for niche-specific information.

Everyday Tools That Can Help You Uncover Original Material

Do you have a contact list? Of course you do, everyone does.

It's just that it may be internal – never having been organized on paper or computer. You may be surprised to find out how many people you do know, directly or indirectly. But what's really shocking when you make such a list is just how diverse your contact list is! It's all good... as this helps generate ideas and establish quick "inside" contacts.

Try making a list of everyone you know. Next to each name, list their profession, favorite hobby, passionate belief, or something you know they're good at and interested in. If you've never done this before, you'll be surprised at the variety of skills, expertise, knowledge and experience that in most cases, is just a phone call or email away.

Build your list of subject area contacts as you go. Continually add to it and you'll have a precious resource ready whenever you need it. When I was a kid my Dad kept a large list of business contacts and acquaintances in a small, pocket-size binder. He referred to this tool as his "brain" because of the irreplaceable value it held in terms of key contact information. You should have seen the chaos that erupted whenever the brain went missing. That's the value of a well-refined list. Back-up copies are strongly recommended however.

Immerse yourself in you subject matter on a daily basis. Go beyond what you already know. Use your current information as a base from which to build.

Discover the key issues the day. Identify the major forces in your area. Really get tuned in to what is going on these days in your area of interest. Be on top of your game and your information will be fresh, up-to-date and well-received.

Listen to the various talk radio shows available related to your general or specific topic. Instead of simply tuning into music every time you get in the car, search the dial for talk-radio. You may find, as I did, a surprising array of guests and topics being discussed at great length.

In the past I've heard interviews and call-in shows with experts on selling on eBay, dating tips, how to buy and sell "fixer-uppers", overpaying child support, and a host of other topics too. In each case, credible sources of information (often the authors themselves) were uncovered and helpful information was openly exchanged. It's just a matter of keeping tuned in and open to what's out there and then gaining something from each experience.

Improve on the Tried and True

Discover an area for much needed improvement and you may have tapped into a potentially profitable topic.

Fast food and pre-packaged meals have become standard fare for many people around the world. These options arose out of a desire to save time and effort, while enjoying a tasty meal. The downside is that these eating habits are clearly unhealthy. It may be routine, accepted as the norm. But what if you could demonstrate how anyone could make healthy meals at home in just minutes?

What about dieting? It's a multi-billion dollar industry that by and large does not work – at least not in the long term. People have been dieting forever... but what if they knew how to make the fundamental shifts that would guarantee an improvement in their overall health?

Take home improvement as another example. Do-it-yourself renovating has taken off in popularity. Big box stores such as Home Depot and Lowes bring formerly hard-to-find supplies directly to the consumer. But how many "weekend carpenters" really know what they're doing? A book on trade secrets and plans ranging from the basic to the more complex could be a big hit. These customers could easily locate some general advice for free, but revealing a step-by-step plan to building an entertainment center, finish a basement, or completely customize a kitchen (and save money at the same time) might be just the thing thousands are looking for.

Bottom line is... information already exists in each of these areas and thousands more. But much of it is based on old information. It may work... but you can spruce it up to make it much better. This is the kind of upgrade and dramatic improvement you should strive for.

Consider any popular book in your subject area. What makes it as winner? Now consider what might be done to make that book even better. Generate enough ideas and you've got the framework for a successful spin-off book.

Ask a better question.

What would make your book, the ultimate, one-stop source for solving not just the symptom of the problem, but the root cause? In other words... what would make your book much more valuable than anything else available on the market today? Look at how things are done now. Has the methodology improved dramatically over the years... or are things still done the same old way? Consider any improvements that are most desirable and base your book on these new and better methods.

Solicit Feedback

If you're a member of the local Chamber of Commerce and you're considering writing a book on small business advertising, seek the opinion of fellow members. You could send out a simple questionnaire to each member asking for feedback, or conduct an informal survey at your next meeting.

You could also post a survey on your website and ask participants on the forums to choose their preferred topic from your short list of possibilities. Ask for contributions and offer a small gift to all or hold a draw from all entries received, with the winner getting a cool gift.

Contributions aren't limited to survey responses. You could solicit content contributors the same way Mark Victor Hansen and Jack Canfield, the authors of the Chicken Soup For The Soul series did.

Invite visitors to your website to share their tips, short stories, insights, examples and life lessons. Offer a token gift or create a competition for the best submission. Just be clear about your intentions and honorable in your actions. Let people know that you're seeking submissions for your book and that any information provided becomes your property. It's worked for others, so there's no reason it won't work for you too.

Fit Your Concept to a Specific Market

Narrow your market and customize your book to suit. Make it industry specific like, Do-It-Yourself Small Business Accounting For Truck Drivers... or Cheap Sleeps Europe: The Definitive Guide to Cheap Accommodation (Katie Wood). It may be that a book offering "Simple But Delicious Cooking For Non-Cooks" would do the trick... or perhaps "The Busy Internet Marketer's Guide To Effective Time Management".

The more specific you can make it, the more your title will appeal to that particular market niche. Narrow it down to a clearly definable audience and you'll naturally pique the attention and interest of that specific group. Since the book addresses them specifically, it possesses magnetic appeal and is therefore more likely to be seen as a "must read" among the targeted group.

Where does your book fit? Is it for beginners, intermediate users, or only the most experienced among us? Target the best audience in your title or sub-title and you'll capture a larger share of that particular market.

Update/ Adapt/ Modernize

Find a past bestseller and create an updated version. Bobbe Summer did this with Pyscho-Cybernetics by Maxwell Maltz. Adapt a popular training course to a book format. Or take an old classic that's in the public domain and modernize it. Many writers are already doing this and there's absolutely no reason why you can't profit from these strategies just the same.

Fit your product to appeal to the market today. Give readers what they want. Make your version more user friendly... fresher, with more bells and whistles... easier to get through... and as current and relevant to today's conditions as it can possibly be.

Tap into the universal desire for achieving desired results quicker and easier. Shape proven concepts to be more relevant to the needs of today's book buyer. Give the buyer the most effective shortcuts. Make yours "new and improved". Show them how to do in 30 days what previously took months or years to learn. Shorten the learning curve and expedite the payoff – that's a sure-fire route to a winning topic.

Some books are almost impossible to find. They sold out their print runs and over the years gained in popularity. Breakthrough Advertising by Eugene Schwartz is such an example. As a copywriter I searched for years to find a used copy at a reasonable price. The last one I located eventually sold for more than $800 US on eBay.

 This resurgence in popularity didn't go unnoticed however as the publisher quickly reprinted the book and sold out all remaining copies near the $100 price point. A quick look on Amazon offered one copy today for $689.

With this kind of book, anyone fortunate enough to own a copy, or anyone with access to a library that still has it could write their own summary of the book and have an instant best-seller among copywriters and marketers.

Let's be clear about this: I'm not talking about stealing material. I'm talking about recasting an old, out-of-print book, and summarizing the key concepts in your own words, thus creating a hybrid product.

I also advise researching the work of other famous names and adding additional perspective to your book. This way you're creating a unique publication while giving people the information they can't currently acquire by any other means.

Never steal someone else's work. What you want to do instead is add value to the marketplace by dusting off ideas and recasting them with new twists, turns and techniques to make them an original and useful piece.

Look At a Problem Through Fresh Eyes

How many books are written solely from the vantage point of the author? As a male, I tend to see things through my eyes alone. So if I was writing a book on building plywood furniture, I might assume that handling large sheets of plywood would be something my readers could easily do on their own.

But that fails to address folks of smaller stature and strength, like many women, as an example. Yet there are more women involved in building trades and home renovation today than ever before. To not consider this segment of the market would limit potential sales. This may not have been a concern in the past but it is reality today.

A better bet might be to begin from a woman's perspective... and supply the information she needs to get the job done. Simply looking at the problem through different eyes can lead to a breakthrough book idea. So if you're stuck, change your viewpoint and consider the subject matter again.

Get inside the mind and heart of your potential buyer. Spend some time in their environment. Learn about the challenges they face and the solutions they desire, as an investigative reporter would. Then... ask yourself... "If I had magic powers, how would I solve this pressing problem my potential buyer is experiencing?" Your answers could trigger your own bestseller.

Chapter 7: Chapter: Planning Your Successful Book... How To Create A Solid Framework To Make Writing Your Book A Breeze

General To Specific

Now it's time to get into the outline – the single most important prerequisite to writing your book. The purpose of your outline is to organize your thoughts and provide a detailed plan of the concepts you're going to discuss in the book.

Before you can craft an outline, you need to narrow your topic down to a single idea. You don't need to finalize the title just yet as the actual cover title you settle on could change as your book takes shape. What we want to do at this point is take your overall subject idea and break it down piece-by-piece until you're left with a detailed plan.

In terms of a visual, think of a funnel. Initially what you're dealing with is broad subject topic. Let's take travel as an example. Travel is a large topic – far too large for any single book. After all, you're not about to write monster tome, but rather a single, specific and targeted volume.

So you need to reduce the general topic of travel down to something more meaningful, direct and specific. One possible way is to narrow the scope geographically. Exploring Canada's West Coast, Student's Travel Guide To Europe, or Must See Sites Of Scandinavia are examples of more narrowly defined topics than "travel". But you can get more specific and still have plenty of material to cover in your book. For example, Exploring Canada's Wild West Coast By Rail is better... as is Student's Essential Travel Guide To Europe On $60 A Day.

Simply reduce your overall subject area and narrow it down like a funnel to create a more specific subject. If you can identify your target market in your book's working title, as in the student travel guide above, that's even better. Your clearly identified audience automatically retains a prominent position this way. This is ideal for both write and reader.

Whatever working title you choose, it's important to keep your niche market in mind while you formulate your outline. That way it's easier to stay on track and keep all content relevant to the audience you're writing for.

If you don't yet have a topic, now is the time to choose something. Kick around numerous possibilities relating to you interests and experience. Brainstorm ideas with a friend. Five minutes of free-wheeling idea generation can produce a long list of possible topics. You'll want to do some market research to test the viability of your concept before your proceed, anyway. So don't get too hung up on making your decision perfect.

Many first-time authors use their professional background as a starting point. That's not a bad way to begin. Now take that specialized expertise and channel into a specific topic you'd like to write about.

Research the Market Potential

Now that you've got a potential subject, it's almost time to start formulating an outline. But first, you want to be reasonably sure your book will succeed from the get-go. While there's no guarantee your book will sell like ice-cold mango lassi's on a blistering hot day in New Delhi, doing some basic research can help put you on the road to success.

If you know your market well, you might have already identified an unattained desire your book can help fulfill, or a problem waiting to be solved.

If you're not so fortunate and you don't feel that you've got your finger on the pulse of your target market, there are some things you can do to test the marketability of your book idea. The primary step should be to get to know who your potential buyers are and how you might be able to reach them.

Consider memberships in associations, publications with readerships that serve your specific market and online discussion forums and lists that cater to the exact people you want to reach. Those are a few good places to start.

Read back issues of industry or special interest newsletter. Find all the ezines and online newsletters that serve your customers. The Directory of Ezines is a valuable guide in this regard, though it's not inexpensive. Another option is to find someone on Fiverr.com (or similar site) that holds a DOE subscription and can compose a list of targeted publications for you.

Print magazines that serve your niche provide another option for uncovering important issues you need to cover in your book. Pay attention to the articles that appear. Editors of such publications know what their readers want to read. They understand the problems and challenges and set out to provide the precise kind of editorial that serves readers and keeps them onboard as paid subscribers.

See how your big idea fits. You might have nailed it in your first attempt. Or, maybe you need to adjust your direction, or even drop the idea altogether. Better to make this discovery before you start writing. Besides, as you learn more about the kind of information that's in demand, topics with huge potential will fall into your lap.

Check the popularity of your subject's keywords online. This helps you gauge the overall interest in the general area. Google's keyword tool is free and its information is as relevant as it gets.

Another terrific source you should check is the Books In Print directory, published by Bowker. Every library has this on hand in print or through online access. It's a large multi-volume collection that lists every book currently in print on every topic imaginable.

Perusing your category and discovering the various titles is time well spent. Making a list of those that capture your interest is a worthwhile exercise. You'll also get an idea of the overall size of the market too.

Don't become discouraged and drop your idea simply because others have written books on your specific topic. Many titles are poorly marketed and die a quiet death. Others may sound like the kind of book you have in mind, but upon closer examination, turn out to be very different in form and content. You may want to locate several books listed and learn more about their contents before choosing your topic and its direction.

Take a moment to review the bestseller lists. Most popular among these lists is Amazon.com and The New York Times bestsellers list. Check other major newspapers too. Large publications often have their own list culled from their sources. Like Books In Print, only published and printed books make it to these lists. But check these out over a period of six months or so and you'll learn the kinds of books that people are buying up in droves.

Self-help, weight loss, diet and exercise, financial and relationship books continue to top the nonfiction charts.

Hundreds, even thousands of books already exist in these general categories. But each year, a fresh new crop of books emerge. So don't let the presence of competing titles stifle your progress. The fact that competitive titles are available means there's a large and hungry market for this type of material.

The advantage of the Amazon bestseller list is its timeliness and size. You won't just get the top 10 or 12 – you get the top 100 books listed and you can search endlessly in any genre. Go through the list and make note of subject areas and titles that tickle your fancy and adjust your plans accordingly.

You can get up-to-the-hour results on the bestsellers of the day at Amazon. It's fascinating to note the relationship between media coverage and sales on Amazon. One appearance on a major television program like 20/20 or Piers Morgan Tonight can sell thousands of books within hours. You may not have heard of a book or its author before. But suddenly they're at the top on Amazon and probably many other lists as well.

Pay attention to media stories and jot down any ideas you can glean from them. A few years back I heard a clip during the business portion of a radio newscast. The story featured the "hottest" trend in online auctions – drop-off centers.

According to the report, new stores were opening up across California to cater to those with merchandise to sell, but without the time or copywriting skills to make it sell on eBay. Customers could simply drop off merchandise which was then sold on consignment for a percentage of the sale price. This got me thinking about eBay and the challenges many people face when listing merchandise for sale and ultimately led to my book on this very topic.

Surveys give your market the opportunity to tell you exactly what they want. If you've got a mailing list of your own, send out a query. Provide a link to your online survey, or send a single page in the mail.

If you don't have a list of your own, consider proposing a joint venture with list owners whose publications reach you potential buyers.

Get creative here. Essentially what you're trying to uncover is the most widespread and significant problem you can solve with the written word. To do so, you need to get your survey out to the afflicted. Consider an exclusive arrangement with a list owner where s/he gets a percentage of sales once your book is done. You might also give them first crack at earning cash from your book through an exclusive pre-publication announcement and offer to their list. Make it worthwhile and you'll find a receptive list owner.

Another way to increase your chances of success is to ride on the coattails of a proven winner. The Celestine Prophecy by James Redfield was a best-seller a number of years ago. It was soon followed by The Celestine Prophecy: An Experiential Guide, The Celestine Prophecy: A Pocket Guide to the Nine Insights, and The Celestine Vision: Living the New Spiritual Awareness. These follow-up books fed off the success of the original – a smart move by the publisher.

Obviously it wouldn't be appropriate or legal to use a name owned by another publisher. But you could certainly feed off of a concept.

Remember the "Pilates" craze a few years ago? Someone got the bright idea of reviving a long-forgotten method of exercise that required little equipment and created a new product. It took off like gangbusters. When I searched Amazon for "Pilates exercise book" – I found literally thousands of different books and information products. Clearly many authors and publishers have cashed in on the craze.

Taking Your Idea and Mapping Out A Book

Okay, so now you've got a solid idea to work with – a clearly defined topic with terrific market potential. Great! That's a solid beginning. Next, it's time to take your topic and turn it into the framework for a book. The way to do that is to create a number of possible chapter topics.

Begin with the most general idea – your book topic – and list the most important and relevant sub-topics. List whatever you think are the most important aspects related to your book's topic.

Let's create a new topic as an example. Here's one -- "Everyday Activities For Burning Fat and Losing Weight Effortlessly".

Possible Chapters...

The basics of burning fat
The value in movement
Reversing society's propensity for laziness
Baby steps that burn off pounds
Losing weight easily
How to protect yourself from gaining it all back
Be aware of the choices you make
The #1 best weight loss exercise
Common pitfalls that keep the pounds on
How to lose weight while you work

Okay... that took about 5 minutes to come up with a list. Surely more subjects could be added or reworded to fit better into the overall concept and intended direction of the book. The point is... in just 5 minutes, we figured out enough chapter topics to create a basic structure of a book.

That's exactly what you should do with your book idea. Spend 5 – 10 minutes coming up with sub-topics on which you could easily write a chapter. To so this... simply ponder these 2 questions:

1. **What's the most important information about this subject?**

2. **What do readers need to know to get maximum benefit from my book?**

To generate the list above, I simply asked these two questions repeatedly while pretending to actually know something about the subject. Obviously you'll be in much better position to write about your selected topic.

More on Mind Mapping

Here's an easy way to free your mind and create potential chapter topics quickly. It's "mind mapping" and it's a method that was first introduced by author and creativity expert, Tony Buzan. Mind mapping is a process for visually mapping out ideas and creating outlines in minutes instead of months. All it takes to create a mind map of your book is a pen, blank sheet of paper and a few minutes time to brainstorm ideas for your book.

The principle behind it all is to stimulate your creativity by engaging the more visually-oriented side of our brain. Mind mapping frees you from any pre-conceived notion of how your outline should appear. Logical thinking tends to be of limited efficiency as ideas are rationalized and then listed in linear fashion. Mind mapping on the other hand is a random and creative idea generation and association process. It's a great way to initiate an outline for any project.

To create a mind map of your book, start with a blank sheet and drawing a bubble in the center of the page. Inside the bubble, list the subject or working title of your book. This is the visual representation or symbol of your total message.

Next, brainstorm key ideas – essential components of your overall theme. These key ideas represent probable chapter topics for your book. Simply list these as keywords all over the page... then frame each in its own bubble... and connect each one to your central concept (title) with a radiating line.

Make your "bubbles" any shape you wish. Rectangles, ovals, triangles, circles, squares, hexagons -- even clouds -- work well. Employ any combination you choose. It's your creation and no one is going to be looking over your shoulder to check out your art skills. Using colored markers helps to identify specific key words. Color also facilitates the easy organization of information while stimulating creative thinking.

At this stage, you know whether you're on the mark and ready to go, or need to refine your focus further.

Think of your book concept or thesis as the top of a table. Each key idea is a leg that supports the tabletop. What are the most significant ideas your reader wants to know? Jot each one down and then think about the next key element related to your topic.

As your mind map takes shape, you'll get a sense about where you stand with respect to this particular topic. If the key ideas flow easily and you've got enough of them (at least 7) it's clear that you can easily proceed to the next step of writing your book.

You can then take your mind map to the next level and fill in the finer details of each major chapter. At this stage, I prefer transferring the information recorded in a mind map to linear format.

Finalize Your Chapter Topics

Take the information from your map on place it on a separate page. This becomes the first page of your book outline. At the top, list your working. If you don't yet have one, use your book's thesis. Take one line to describe what you're book will offer – clearly and simply.

Next, list all the keywords from your mind map. These are the main ideas and concepts that are high-probability chapter topics for your book. List one item per line, until you've transferred all the major ideas to this new page.

Here's what this one page outline might have looked like for author Deepak Chopra's book -- The Seven Spiritual Laws of Success: A Practical Guide to the Fulfillment of Your Dreams:

Law of Pure Potentiality
Law of Giving
Law of Cause & Effect
Law of Least Effort
Law of Intention & Desire
Law of Detachment
Law of Purpose in Life

Now think of the most crucial information you could share. Are any big ideas missing from this list? If so, add them immediately. You want to be sure to include everything the reader needs to extract maximum benefit from your work. Include every key factor that will help the reader play their desired role or solve their troubling problem.

Once you're convinced the major issues have been identified and listed, it's time to put them in order. What chapter should be your first? The best advice I can give is to organize your ideas in the **most logical way**.

Prioritize your chapters any of the following ways:

From the general to the specific

From the first step in the process to the last

From the most important to the least

From the "tried and true" to the "new and improved"

From the earliest event to the most recent

From A to Z

There's no "one size fits all" rule here. You have a good idea of what you're going to say in your book.

Now you just need to organize your main ideas in a way that makes the most sense. A reader-friendly approach is always your best bet. You don't want to confuse anybody or have them struggle to grasp your information. So simply start at the beginning with the most logical starting point. Then proceed to the next, most logical step in the sequence.

The more chapter topics you have, the more there is to organize. Don't let it stress you out. At this point, all you need is a rough idea of the overall sequence you'll use to deliver the information.

Once the writing is complete, you can easily juggle things around. But having a sequence in mind from the beginning helps you deliver the content in the most effective way for the reader.

How Your Detailed Outline Serves You

A quality outline is without a doubt, the most valuable tool in the writer's arsenal. It keeps you moving in the right direction and prevents you from meandering off in a direction you didn't plan on from the beginning.

It takes some time and effort to create a detailed outline, to be sure. But once completed, you have an original document that can lead to your pot of gold.

The outline is the heart and soul of your book. Without it, your book is nothing but a dream. But take your big idea and develop it into a comprehensive outline and you give it shape, purpose and meaning.

In essence, your outline is every important bit of information and insight you're going to share in the book. It's all there before you in black and white and it will shave months of time off the writing of your work. Most importantly, it makes the writing process an absolute delight – as you'll soon discover.

A detailed outline forces you to think upfront – so you don't have to slow down once you're on a roll. There's no stopping to figure out what to say next. You simply go on to the next point or the next segment and continue writing. Once you start writing, the words flow as if by magic. It's all been thought through and organized. All you have to do now is compose a bunch of sentences.

Outlining is the major key to getting your book done in the least amount of time and without any major snags along the way. It's the number one secret for turning anyone into a proficient writer. You might find this difficult to believe and I understand where you're coming from if you do. But just give it a sincere effort and you too will be singing the praises of creating a detailed outline in advance.

Preparing an outline before you write is a hardly a new technique. It's where you think through all the ideas you want to write about and then you organize them in point form.

When you're ready to write, you start writing at any point you like. No one said you had to begin with page one and continue sequentially to the end. **Start with the chapter that looks most appealing to you.** You can always go back and complete previous chapters a little later.

Create an Outline for One Chapter at a Time

Okay, so you've got your topic and major chapters figured out. The next step is to transform each of your chapter titles into a detailed chapter outline. Once you've completed this step you'll be able to write a 10 to 20 page chapter with ease.

Start by listing keywords or phrases pertaining to the chapter topic. If you've got a possible chapter heading in mind, by all means list it at the top of the page. You want to be crystal clear about the direction and purpose of the chapter, but you can always add or modify the title later on.

The main idea I want to drive home is this: clearly and succinctly articulate your chapter topic and write it down at the top of the page. You can use a single key word, or a sentence to summarize the content of this particular chapter. The secret is to focus and the more clearly defined the subject matter, the easier it is to focus and generate outstanding and highly-relevant content.

Write your chapter concept or thesis and then add the specific details.

Number the lines down the page from 1-10, leaving a space between each line. Next, write down the most significant ideas, techniques, concepts, tactics, methods, or insights that relate to the topic and would fit well in this chapter.

If your chapter is about making bread at home the old fashioned way, start listing the big ideas you learned about the process. This might include essential tools, key ingredients, baker's secrets, health benefits of homemade bread, etc. List everything that comes to mind and give yourself whatever time you need to fill up 10 lines. You can always increase this number or add extra chapters if you've got more content to include.

If you can only think of a few ideas, ask yourself repeatedly the 2 magic questions used evolve your chapter topics:

1. What's the most important information about this subject?
2. What do readers need to know to get maximum benefit from my book?

Keep writing down those flashes of insight until you fill up the page. Once you've uncovered all you can with the 2 questions above, ask the journalists questions. Simply consider who, what, why, where, when and how to flesh out additional content as needed.

Start each question with one of these words and fill in the blanks.

Who made bread this way? Who developed this technique and why? What are the important things to remember about bread-making? Why should health-conscious parents consider making their own bread? Where can you find rare ingredients? How do you knead dough... and how can you tell when it's ready for the oven?

So how easy it is?

Just create a bunch of questions that fit and add them to your chapter outline. Most of the information will not only be usable, but will make for some very interesting content readers will enjoy and appreciate.

Ask yourself the kind of questions a curious and interested reader would like to know.

Start with the important ideas you already had in mind. Then use the question method to fill out the page. If you can't come up with 10 good ideas, don't fret about it. If you've got 5 gems, that's just fine. If you only have a couple, try combining this content with another chapter.

Keep your chapter concept at the top of the page and you'll stay on track. Each sub-topic you add should relate to the chapter. This ensures that your content will be easily processed by the reader.

The next step is to review your chapter sub-topics for relative importance.

Remember, you want to give your reader the best, most relevant material without any filler. So each sub-topic needs to justify itself. Either it's important to the reader or it isn't. Anything not considered important and necessary should be deleted from your chapter outline.

If you started with 10 sub-topics and then reviewed each one, you might only have 7 key ideas of merit to share with your readers. If your list holds 12 sub-topics, maybe only 10 of those are really important. 10 is a good round number to shoot for – particularly with your first book. It is possible that everything you've listed is valuable information. And you can always relocate some sub-topics elsewhere.

At this point, you have your book concept, main chapter topics and a basic chapter outline for one chapter. You'll want to fill in the same kind of detail for each and every chapter. But before you do, I suggest completing your chapter outline in detail, by taking it one step further.

Now's the time to fill in the details for each sub-topic listed in your chapter outline. Take a quick look at the topic and write down whatever comes to mind. Keep your focus on providing key information to the reader. Think of the most important details your reader needs to know about each sub-topic.

Again it's time to ask the 2 magic questions:

What's the most important information about this subject? What does my reader need to know to derive maximum benefit from this book?

And I'm going to add a third question at this point...

How can I demonstrate or illustrate this point?

Don't get wordy here. Record whatever thoughts, key words, and examples come to mind. If you had to detail this sub-topic in just a handful of words – what would those words be?

Shoot for 3-5 short-form details about each sub-topic. When you run dry, it's time to ask those who, what, where, why, when and how questions again. Just begin asking a question with one of these words and insert any appropriate ending. Add your point form answers in the designated area. Do this for each sub-topic in the chapter. But only spend a few minutes in each area. Doing so will allow you to crank out a very detailed and complete chapter outline in short order.

Another approach is to think of any action words you can plug in to use as triggers to help uncover additional supporting points.

Once you've completed one chapter... repeat this process for the others. I know it sounds like a lot of work, but believe me when I tell you that this will be the most important work you ever do – as far as your book is concerned. If you don't see it yet, hang in there – you will.

*Note: if you use one page for each chapter as I prefer, you'll need to write your details in very small print. If this is too difficult or distracting for you, consider adding extra spaces between each sub-topic, and pages to your outline. It's important to use these ideas... but it's equally important that you adjust them to best suit your style.

Use whatever outlining tools you prefer. If you're used to using legal pads for your work, then buy all means, use them for your outline. If extending your chapter outline over numerous pages doesn't bother you, go for it. I'm simply sharing the tools and techniques that work best for me and one such technique is to fit the outline for an entire chapter on a single page. I find this helps me maintain focus and direction amidst the inevitable daily interruptions. It's easy to step back in and pick up where I left off.

Once you've detailed each chapter to this extent, staple all the pages together and mark the front in color so it's impossible to lose. Don't forget the initial page listing the various chapters of our book. This ensures that you have a brief overview of the book right before your eyes. You now have your completed outline in hand. With this document, you're just days away for the completion of your book.

The Next Step – Writing Your Book

Now that your outline is complete, it's time to start writing. Dive in and get started.

The easiest way to get moving is to pick your favorite chapter. Some chapters tend to appeal more than others. But if you quickly review your outline, you'll notice one or two chapters just bursting with information. This is the kind of chapter you'll find easiest to write – so start there.

When it's this appealing, the odds are overwhelmingly in your favor that digging in will truly be a satisfying experience. It's the best way to get your writing off to a amazing start.

If you've held the notion that a book should be written from front to back, now would be a good time to dispel the myth. Writing is easiest when you feel comfortable with the raw material in front of you.

To write a chapter, start with one segment. Then move to another. Continue along in this fashion until the chapter is complete. Writing one chapter at a time is an effective and efficient way to get your book finished fast.

With each sub-topic, allow a maximum of 10 minutes writing time. Get yourself a timer. The one I use is a simple battery-operated device with an alarm. I simply program the timer for 10 minute intervals, click the button and start writing using the details listed under each sub-topic.

The trick is to write continuously for those 10 minutes. If you're blessed with even average speed on the keyboard, you can expect to complete anywhere from ½ page to a full page of text in just 10 minutes.

Try it and you'll see for yourself. For some people, 10 minutes may be too much time to cover what needs to be said in the segment. What I suggest is starting with 10 minute segments and adjusting the timeframe accordingly to suit. 10 minutes works best for me, but you might find another magic number that yields maximum production and gets your back completed that much sooner. Don't get too crazy here. Spend a minimum of 5 and a maximum of 20 minutes on each sub-topic.

Do this consistently and you'll be pleasantly surprised at your level of production. At times it will feel as though your book practically writes itself.

Write as fast as you can for the designated time. Include the important details and key words. If you can add an example or effective analogy, do so. But don't stop writing for those 10 minutes, or whatever time you've assigned to each small segment.

Not only will the speed at which you write surprise you and help you get your book completed that much sooner, you'll also write better.

This may be difficult to accept, as it was for me. The only way you'll truly be convinced is to put this concept to the test for yourself.

When you absolutely, positively MUST get it done in 10 minutes – you will.

But... when you get used to the idea that all you can spend on one segment is ten minutes, you will soon focus like you never have before.

When you become accustomed to hearing the timer sound and then moving on regardless, if compels you to communicate in the most direct and effective way. There are no wasted words. No long, drawn out stories. No exchange of pleasantries. No long-winded wind-up. No thinking about other issues while you stare out your window.

You simply say what needs to be said in the most expedient way possible. It's maximum production and word efficiency.

Take full ownership of each sub-topic for the allotted time. Convert each one into a segment. So if you've listed 10 sub-topics for your chapter, you'll write 10 different segments – allowing 10 minutes for each.

At this pace, you can write your entire 10-segment chapter in one hour and forty minutes, if you wrote continuously. I suggest you include a couple of 10 minute breaks as well for each chapter you write.

After writing 4 or 5 segments, take a short rest. Get up from your chair and stretch a little. Take in a little fresh air and sunshine if you can. Pour yourself a steaming cup of Starbucks French Roast, or whatever beverage satisfies your soul. Then get ready for another session of productive writing.

Take a brief moment before triggering your timer again. Get comfortable in your chair. Wiggle your fingers to keep then nimble – and smile because you're on your way!

Then take a look at the one specific sub-topic you're going to write about over the next 10 minutes. Review the brief details you filled in earlier including any relevant key words. This entire process should take about 30 seconds. If you're spending much more time this you're impeding your progress and interrupting the natural flow.

Okay, once you're ready to roll, launch the timer and start writing. Do not let up until it sounds again.

Write whatever comes to mind. Let your brain go to work on turning the details into sentences. Don't pay any attention to style or grammar. Don't wonder if you're making sense or not. Just get it all out there quickly. Make your point and then move on to the next point.

Keys To Creating Segments Your Readers Will Love

Sell your ideas. Use whatever factual information you have at your disposal and speak with conviction. Demonstrate your point with poignant examples when it's appropriate to do so. Convince the reader that your information and methods work and work well.

Take the raw material collected at the outline stage and recast it in sentence form. Forget perfect English. Just say it as directly – complete with tone variance, animation and a sense of vibrancy. Let your ideas flow forth with a sense of aliveness.

Communication is the key. You've got key information to share with your reader. In order to transfer your insights and experience efficiently... you've simply got to get it out.

Just say what needs to be said as you would conversationally. If you had mere minutes to tell a friend about your brilliant discovery, you wouldn't waste any time on the irrelevant or superfluous. You'd get right to the point and communicate in clear words as directly as you possibly could. That's the exact kind of communication you want to achieve in writing your segments.

Take what you've got and present it as interestingly as possible.

Mix up your sentence lengths. Toss in the odd one-word sentence – it stands out and compels readers to read on. Forget proper form. Simply write as you'd speak. Your mission is to convey the most significant information about that particular sub-topic. So... write it as you'd say it. You'll see how easy it is one you get rolling.

Details Make the Difference

Quality outlining is the key to swift and easy writing. You'll make this discovery sooner or later as you progress through the various chapters of your book.

With an abundance of material to work with, the actual writing is child's play. But once you've exhausted what you have and you still find yourself short, it's much more difficult to continue.

Details are the key to effortless writing.

With abundant facts, key words, analogies or examples, you'll constantly be pressed to fit it all into one tiny 10-minute segment. This is exactly what you want. Even though you may find it a little frustrating in the beginning, over the long haul, you'll discover the value for yourself.

Having more to work with than you'll ever need gives you options. To make your book as good as can be you'll want to share the very best detail with readers. Prioritize your information so you're always starting with the juicy information first. This way, should the clock run out before you get to share it all, you can wrap up the segment confident in the knowledge that you've revealed the most important and useful information to your readers.

Adequately outlined segments make for easy, breezy writing. But you don't need lots of written detail in your outline to have plenty of material to shape into sentence form. That's why I only leave one blank space after each sub-topic in the outline.

Having too words in your outline is self-defeating. You want to be able to grasp the subject matter of each section at a glance. The best way to do this is to use short, point-form notes and key words as triggers. These launching pads allow you to explode into colorful, descriptive prose – making the writing effortless and the finished product interesting and effective.

How To Make Your Writing Come Alive

Power words, illustrative examples and perfectly positioned quotations help make your writing more interesting and expressive. I'm not suggesting you use a big $100 word when the 50¢ variety does the job. Simple language works best. But you can add color and flavor with a sprinkling of words that capture eyeballs, intrigue, arouse interest and convey a meaning that's instantly understood.

Action words and occasional questions keep the reader involved and moving right along. They also provide a slight change of pace to keeps things interesting.

Descriptive words and phrases help paint a clearer picture. On-target illustrations help you make your point and drive home the information in dramatic fashion.

Mix it up as you would in an intense discussion with your best friend. Be as expressive as you need to be to communicate your ideas.

Get Into Peak State

Here's another secret to effortless writing. Get into a positive state of mind before attempting to put words on the page.

Peak mental and emotional states produce wonderful passages that flow as naturally as a mountain stream. But try writing amidst personal turmoil or when dozens of distractions are calling out to you simultaneously and you'll only get frustrated and whatever you create will likely get trashed later.

If you don't feel like writing – don't. That might sound ridiculous since this very text is about helping you write your book in the shortest amount of time. But let me explain. If you're not feeling up to it, you won't be giving your reader your best effort – that's the bottom line. And if it's not your best, do you really want to put your name on it? Sure... you want to get the darned thing done – every writer does. But make it something you can be proud of and the payoff will last for many years.

What if you never feel like writing?

Well, I think there are some deeper issues at play like the fear of failure. But if you fully intend to follow through and get your best effort completed and out there in the marketplace, you're going to have to push yourself to work a little bit each day towards that goal.

Deal with pressing distractions. If they're urgent, you simply cannot ignore them for long. Who needs that kind of pressure anyway?

Find a time when you can be alone with your thoughts and your computer. For me the optimum time is the early hours of the morning. At this time, no one's going to call or knock on the door. It's a peaceful time. No matter what else is going on throughout the rest of day, I can almost always find an hour to devote to my book writing.

When you're not feeling up to it, change my focus by imagining the book already completed and selling like crazy. Visualize all the wonderful comments from enthusiastic readers and imagine your growing bank account. Know in your heart that the only way this can happen is if you follow through on your plan and get your book written.

A writing partner or coach can also be a tremendous advantage, providing words of encouragement and inspiration at the precise time you need it most. If you need a little extra support, or someone to bounce ideas off, you can always contact me. I love my readers and I want nothing more than to see you succeed.

You should be in a positive frame of mind before you begin to write. Ideally you want to feel energetic, vibrant, and alive before you write a word. You have every reason to feel enthusiastic and upbeat about the prized information you have to share.

By the time you're ready for the actual writing, you've already become an authentic expert on your subject. You've done your research and uncovered precious information readers are certain to find helpful. If you weren't capable of producing a terrific book on this very subject, you would never have come this far. Know that you have what it takes to pull it off. Now start writing and build on your momentum. Soon you'll become an unstoppable force and your book will be done exactly as you planned.

Chapter Eight: Strategies For Writing a Great Book FAST

Make Your Book a Priority

Priorities take precedence. You're obviously serious about writing your book. So make it a must that you follow through and get it done.

When you absolutely, positively know that your book will be completed and that it's just a matter of days, the universe conspires to assist you. Unusual circumstances and events seem to happen out of the blue. That perfect quotation you've been looking for suddenly appears. The name of an expert comes to mind who will give you a superb interview if you only ask for it. A particularly relevant and timely report is mysteriously handed to you by a friend.

Once you've made the commitment, those things you need are mysteriously made available to you. It's not that they weren't there all along... it's that you never noticed them before. But once you accept without question that your book is being written – for all intents and purposes, it already has.

Make a commitment to completion and blockages are quickly dissolved.

Don't just tell yourself you're going to write a book – make it declaration and see it as already having been accomplished. This isn't some obscure theory, it's a universal law applied to book writing.

Make a contract with yourself. Following through won't just give you a book – it will turbo-charge your self-esteem and quite possibly, change your life in many new and exciting ways.

Gather Ample Information

Assemble your collected knowledge prior to any writing. Take an inventory of what you've got and determine what is still needed.

Insist on a solid foundation of information and expertise before you start writing. If you're lacking in any key areas, find the experts who can help you fill in the blanks via an interview.

You want your book to be taken seriously and you want people to come away with a good feeling about you. Build on established, proven principles and methods. Add your own unique experiences, insights, improvements, and spin and you'll have an outstanding product.

Give Readers Your Best Information

Openly share your inside secrets, closely-guarded shortcuts and tricks of the trade. Concentrate your efforts on providing the best, most comprehensive and complete information anywhere. Give your reader the kind of inside scoop she secretly desires but has little hope of unearthing herself.

Let readers in on your discoveries. Share your perspective and personal observations and insights. Give the kind of detailed information only and insider could provide. Do this and readers will devour every word and you'll sell plenty of copies of your book.

Take your information and simplify it. Allow the reader to get up to speed in the shortest conceivable time. Shorten the learning curve by focusing on only the key information and avoid the extraneous material they'll easily find elsewhere.

Saving your reader time and sparing them the frustrations you encountered along the way is exactly the kind of detail you want to supply. Such is the stuff that makes a great book and a sound investment for the buyer. Keep them interested by sharing the most significant information on each sub-topic. Give value above all.

Deliver the methods and techniques that will make life easier and happier for readers. Help them get what they want faster, with fewer hassles. Offer solutions that deliver instant or near-instant gratification. The quicker the payoff – the more appeal your product has over others.

Keep Your Reader in Mind

It's easy to get carried away on go off on a wild tangent. You know people who do this when they speak. They're the type who never shut up. They go on and on about anything so intent on "speaking" that they fail to notice their audience has drifted away. This is exactly the approach you must avoid.

Following your outline and sticking to time-limited writing segments helps you stay on course and deliver your best information on each page. But there's another way to guarantee that your content is relevant to the audience: keep your reader in mind as you write - always.

Sounds obvious, doesn't it?

But getting sidetracked is a common problem that's easily avoidable by keeping an image of your reader in the forefront of your mind.

Communicate directly about something of genuine interest and importance to your reader, as you would in a face-to-face conversation.

You want your words to have impact – to produce a result. In order to achieve this, your words must be heard and understood. Your best bet is to begin with a solid understanding of your readers. Know the problems, challenges, and obstacles they face... and never forget the results they desire. If you consistently move towards that end – you're on the right track.

Keep your reader in mind as you go and you'll find it easier to communicate on their level. You'll find yourself assembling words and concepts in the most meaningful context -- one's that's easy for the audience to grasp.

Use Stories, Metaphors and Analogies

Every page of your book should contain content that is instantly understood the first time. Simplify your concepts to match your reader's level of understanding and deliver your information in a context that aids and solidifies their comprehension. In short, make every effort to facilitate reader understanding.

Examples work well. So too do metaphors, analogies and interesting stories. Use any of these to help drive home important points throughout your book and it makes for a more interesting learning experience.

There's no need to go overboard with your stories, metaphors and analogies. Use as needed to drive home your point, but don't add extra words just to fill up the page.

Hint at the Good Stuff Still to Come

Anticipation builds enthusiasm. Give all you've got in each chapter and then tease the reader about something that's coming up... something you know they'll enjoy or find particularly helpful.

Setting the scene in this way arouses curiosity and stimulates interest, making it more likely your book buyer will continue reading, rather than putting the book down.

The sooner your reader gets through your book, the sooner she can apply the information and attain the desired results. Allow readers to easily devour your book by enticing them to read on rather than retire for the evening. Even if they don't do so right away, you can bet they'll get back to your book at the earliest opportunity because you've planted the seed and heightened their level of curiosity and interest.

With high expectations of future content and their enthusiasm bubbling over, delighted readers are quick spread the word about your book, generating additional sales. This is a win-win situation and a by-product of creating a quality book that truly helps readers in some way. When your buyer reads your book faster, they stand to gain all the benefits sooner. Word quickly spreads, boosting your sales as you've gained another ally. But it doesn't end there. Happy buyers often anxiously wait for your next book on a related topic, giving you a surge of instant sales upon its release.

Involve the Senses

When you're forced to write quickly, you tend to write as you'd speak. Conversational English works wonders when converted to the printed page. Just open up and let your personality spill out onto the page. Write the way you'd say it.

One of the keys to effective writing is to involve all of your senses. Write so readers can see it, hear it, and feel what you share. Some readers are primarily visual and translate words into pictures. Others are more hearing oriented. Still others interpret words mostly through feelings. Express yourself freely and vividly. Encompass the full dimension of human experience as it relates to your sub-topic and you'll touch more people with your information.

Use colorful language, creative metaphors and convey your ideas as only you can. That's one way you can be sure of producing 100% original material.

Show your spark. Let the words flow unencumbered. Be who you are and let the folks in your market niche reap the rewards of your insights, experiences and simple explanations.

Emulate Your Best, Most Intense Conversations

With every sub-topic you tackle, your purpose is to deliver the BIG ideas quickly and efficiently. It's about getting your point across clearly, effectively and efficiently. Write with the same kind of passion you'd use to argue your viewpoint in a deep personal conversation.

"The mind is not a vessel to be filled but a fire to be kindled." -- Plutarch

You wouldn't stop to think about your delivery, yet chances are you'd be masterful in its execution. Why? Simply because you've got something meaningful to say... something that's right and true in your heart... something that fuels your passion... and it's something that needs to be said.

Want to write more powerfully?

Simply emulate your performance in conversational debate. Feel your voice shining through. Note the variations in tone and timbre. Make the gestures you'd make in person to more forcefully communicate your point. Do this and your writing will be energized with a renewed sense of purpose and meaning.

Give Yourself Permission

Let freedom reign. These are just words from a famous speech – they're words every writer should live by.

Freedom allows your writer's voice to emerge. It unlocks the chains that restrict and limit what you'd really like to say when you're totally free to speak your mind.

No one's going to see your material until much later and only after you've approved of it. So have no fear about what you write. Just let it out. Get it down. Move on the next thought and keep going forward. Give yourself permission to explode into prose. When you bear down and write freely for 10 minutes at a time, you'll amaze even your harshest critic. You forget that you're writing as the words, concepts and fresh new details and perspectives come to you with incredible frequency.

Just let yourself go. Write like crazy. You never have to wonder – "Should I, or shouldn't I include this?" Just get it down. You can always remove it later, if need be. But most of the time, that won't be necessary as the section in question adds life to your text, more often than not.

You don't have to worry about going wayward – your outline keeps you channeled in the direction you want to go. But give yourself permission to write whatever comes to mind and you'll produce interesting and lively copy. It's 100 times more interesting than the stifled and stuffy work that comes from attempting to "write" in a formal manner.

Let Your Creative Mind Direct Your Fingers

Familiarize yourself with the concept upon which you are about to write. Momentarily immerse yourself in the sub-topic and the details you've included in your outline. Then take a deep breath, close your eyes and allow those ideas to form an image in your mind. See the miniature lesson unfold in your mind's eye. This whole process should only take about 30 seconds or so.

Then set your timer and get busy writing. Describe the picture you just visualized. See it and then write it. Share the lesson as clearly and directly as you can.

Write non-stop. Have faith in yourself and trust in the process. As a thought enters your consciousness, put it into a sentence. As examples come to mind, include them if you can, or make note of the example and go back to it later.

After a few segments, you'll notice how easy it is to write powerful sections of a nonfiction book. The words flow automatically and effortlessly as you enter into that zone of peak productivity. At this point, it doesn't feel much like "work" at all. The heavy lifting was already done at the outline stage. Now, you're merely expressing yourself. The keyboard is simply a recording device to capture your thoughts.

Say whatever is on your mind. Share your special lessons, stories, secrets and shortcuts learned from your personal experience. Explain yourself clearly and succinctly. Communicate with passion and your readers will be glad they invested in your book.

Utilize Unique Experiences

Open up your mind and heart. Be willing to share personal observations, case histories, individual experiences and chance encounters. It means exposing a little bit about yourself – who you are and where you've been. In the beginning, it might be a little uncomfortable. But the more human interest you can add to your book, the more compelling and unique it becomes.

No one else has experienced the subject quite the same way. It's this one of a kind perspective that gives your book added value and sovereignty.

Free Yourself From The Pressure To Write

Forced writing isn't any fun. And the result it generates usually isn't any good anyway.

Your book is your project and no one else's. No one's holding a gun to your head and demanding that you spend countless hours cranking out page after page. But I'm willing to but that if you were forced at gunpoint to write your book in 10 days – you'd do it. A little leverage can be a good thing. But overdoing it can stifle the best of intentions.

I've mentioned a few times that the methods shared here will help you write your book in 30 days. But the truth is – it can be done much faster. 30 days is the maximum time to invest in your book project. Once your outline is completed and the writing begins, you gain momentum and you'll astound yourself by your ability to get it done in a lot less time.

If you're feeling any pressure to write, step back for a moment. Take a bird's eye view of the situation. Examine the root of the problem and you'll discover that all the pressure and anxiety you're feeling is essentially self-induced.

If you're struggling to get the first few pages written, maybe you've allowed yourself to become overwhelmed by it all. Perhaps it's time to step back, regroup and rework your plan so you can complete one segment, chapter or section at a time.

Set smaller daily goals and make a commitment to their completion. Do this for several days in a row and you'll be well on your way to having your book written and published.

If a 10 minute timeframe for each segment causes performance anxiety, change it accordingly. Just be sure to follow through by consistently – writing non-stop for the duration – whatever time period works for you. Just don't be afraid to push yourself. Those early frustrations are merely the seeds of growth and transformation.

It's easy to write using this system. All you're doing is connecting the dots.

Essentially, it's just a matter of taking the framework you structured into an outline and filling in the blanks. Take it one step and one at a time. Use the details you've already listed and form them into sentences. Write continuously until the timer sounds and don't look back. Constant advancement brings you to the finish line every time.

Chapter Nine: Chapter: Speed Writing Tips, Techniques & Strategies

Always Work From Your Outline

You've heard this before but it's so crucial to you nonfiction writing success that it bears repeating. Always construct an outline before attempting to write your book.

Perhaps you consider yourself naturally creative or a gifted writer. Or maybe like many, you haven't written much of anything since school. It doesn't really matter where you fit in on the scale of experience. Not starting with a detailed outline will eventually pin you into a corner forcing you to throw up your hands in utter frustration.

Even the best, most skilful and commercially successful writers outline their work before actually creating it.

Whether your next book is your first or your thirty-first, taking the time to construct a workable outline first should be your number one priority. Everything else about your book is secondary in my opinion.

Don't be tempted into writing your book because you're "feeling" it. Assemble an outline first and make it your detailed blueprint. I guarantee it will make the process far easier, the product much stronger, and you'll get your book done that much faster.

Remember to keep it simple. You don't need an elaborate plan that takes months to complete. In fact, if it takes you too long to fill in the details, you run the risk of never completing your book. Keep it simple and straightforward. The best outline is one you can pick up at any time, browse through and then start writing a particular segment from any chapter.

Mind maps work well for quickly establishing your book's concept and supporting chapters. It's a quick, direct route to formulating and refining a specific topic.

Keep your map to a single page and you'll have an overview of your book as a reference while you fill in the more detailed elements of your outline.

All it takes is a few short minutes to create a visual mind map. The result is a shell or framework you can develop further. It's a simple method for launching your outline rapidly. With this solid framework in hand, refining your ideas, organizing your thoughts and filling in details becomes a quick and painless task.

Direct Your Mind.... Then Let It Take Over

Your outline is the roadmap to take you where you want to go. It's what gives your writing specific direction and meaning. It's the background material – the ingredients you'll use to cook up a terrific book. Your outline points you in the right direction and provides the fuel to get you there. It's your collection of facts, ideas and examples – the very substance of non-fiction content.

Trust yourself and your outline. You've done the necessary work. Now when you sit down to write, let your mind take over.

Say it your way. Don't wonder if it's the absolute best way – simply communicate the information as directly as you can. Give yourself total freedom of expression and let your mind take over. The outline gives you a channel and a direction. But the magic comes through when you free your spirit and make way for your authentic voice.

Let It Flow

Use your fingers on the keyboard to capture the presentation of material your mind churns out. Type away and capture it all. Whatever comes to mind goes on the page immediately. Let it flow continuously and you'll be pleasantly surprised with the outcome.

Speed writing is about getting as many thoughts recorded as possible within the time allotted to each section. The only way you can cover what you want to say in 10 short minutes is to let your words flow freely without disruption.

Let your fingertips follow your mind as the conduit of expression. Don't stop to re-read or ponder your next statement. Keep moving forward and both the volume and quality of content will amaze and delight you.

Reward Yourself For Your Accomplishments

What's the best way to motivate another person to do what you want? Offer an incentive – a reward in exchange for action. Well, it works the exact same way when the reward is self-administered.

Challenge yourself to go for it – to reach for that new plateau. But make it even more enticing and you'll find pockets of opportunity that suddenly present themselves to help you get what you want sooner, rather than later.

Holding your completed book in hand is reward enough for many. But the sheer number of blank pages can for some make it seem like an impossibly long journey. So it doesn't hurt to dangle another big and juicy carrot before your eyes and promise it to yourself upon the successful completion of your book.

As humans, we're most often driven by the potential payoff. When the promise of reward far outweighs the investment in time, energy, or expense, we are much more likely driven towards action.

Reward yourself for a job well done and keep the reward front and center in your mind. Look for small ways to treat yourself as you make daily progress on your book. Do the work first and then allow yourself to indulge in something you thoroughly enjoy. It can give you that extra burst of energy when you need it most.

Write In Time-Limited Segments

Limiting the amount of time you spend writing each sub-section does wonders for your productivity. Get used to this method of covering one idea in 5 to 10 minute segments and then quickly moving on to the next.

When you first try this approach, the timer might seem a bit imposing and intimidating. At first you'll feel rushed – maybe even somewhat panicky about the whole situation as you scramble to cover the sub-topic at hand.

But eventually and inevitably – you'll come to appreciate the timer. It's your best friend as far as productive writing goes. What it does is drive you, compelling you to scribble down your ideas at a furious pace. It's the best method I've found for generating content at warp speed.

Try it and you'll see. What at first seems annoying, is actually a valuable ally, forcing direct, to the point communication without any filler. Play around with various timeframes and settle on the one that works best for you.

7-minute segments work well for me. In just 7 minutes, I can easily write one half to one full page of text. This means that if my chapter consists of 10 segments, I'll need 70 minutes of hard-core writing time to get it done. Once completed, I'll have a 5 to 10 page chapter written. Not a bad return on investment. Use this system of writing in time-limited segments and you'll be delighted with your increased efficiency and quality of writing.

Write Often

If you're serious about wanting to write a book, write something at every opportunity. The best training for writing is to write regularly. It doesn't really matter what kind of gibberish you write. Just write something. Write whenever you get a free moment and you'll soon find it effortless to write when you really need to.

Set aside time each day to work on your book. It's best if you can schedule it at a peaceful hour when you're at your peak state – mentally and physically.

If you can write a chapter a day and your outline consists of 12 chapters, you'll have your book written in less than two weeks.

If all you think you can squeeze in is one sub-topic per day and your outline features 85 sub-topics in total, you'll still get your book written in less than 3 months. Find a way to write 3 tiny segments a day (anyone can do this) and you'll knock your book out in less than a month.

Could you spare 10 minutes a day creating something that could make your money for years to come? Of course you can! But let's be honest here: Is 10 minutes all you possibly fit in to your schedule? If you really tried, could you devote a half-hour or more to your book project? Think about it. The sooner you turn it out, the sooner you can enjoy all the rewards.

Repetition develops skill and positive habits. The more frequently you write, the better it gets and the easier it becomes to write again. You'll no longer be intimidated by any writing project.

Remember, a book is nothing more than a series of individual sections or segments. After conquering your first book, imagine how easy it will be to write an article or short report. In writing one hundred or more individual segments, you gain new skills, experience and confidence in your writing ability. As your skill and confidence level increases, you begin to look for additional opportunities to write.

To get your book finished in a short period of time, try writing one chapter every day. This is the target I often shoot for. I don't always reach it, but in making a serious effort each day, I know I'm progressing steadily towards completion.

Each time you dig into your project and write, you're fanning the flames of enthusiasm. The more often you pick it up and craft another segment, the more you'll look for additional opportunities to do so and the sooner your book is a done deal.

For me, there's no better time to write than first thing in the morning, while the house is quiet. When I purposely wake-up an hour or two earlier, I know I'll be pleased with my accomplishments before the regular workday even begins.

Some people are "night owls" preferring to stay up long after most have called it a night. If this works for you, use your "after hours" time to write your book. In just one hour of super-productive writing each night, you'll easily finish your book ahead of schedule.

Bring Your Book To Life Through The Spoken Word

Just the thought of writing can be intimidating or paralyzing to some people. Perhaps it's the long-lasting effect of deep-seated memories of assignments, essays, exams, and teachers with a preponderance of writing rules. Think "writing" and unnecessary limitations tend to appear for a lot of people and that's a shame.

If traditional writing is a challenge for you, it's best to forget about the challenges and simply "speak" your book into existence instead. "Speaking" supersedes those limiting rules of writing. You're simply communicating in a down-to-earth, off the cuff style.

Transferring the images that flow from your mind to the page is what writing is all about. For most, the preferred method for accomplishing this is the keyboard. But you can also speak your thoughts into a microphone and have your words appear in written form.

There are two ways you can do this:

1. Use a voice-to-text software program like Dragon Naturally Speaking or...

2. Have someone else transcribe your spoken word recording into text.

Each option has its advantages and disadvantages. Software involves a cash investment, learning curve and training time.

Transcription involves selecting a capable service provider and a cash investment. If your plans are to only write one book – the transcription solution would probably make more sense. But you should choose the method that works best for you if you want an alternate to creating books the traditional way.

Develop a Laser-Like Focus

Maximum concentration equals maximum output. Writing isn't like production-line product assembly where habitual routines can be carried out without much conscious thought or attention.

Writing demands a continuous focus. You can't mentally take a trip to some foreign beach and still crank out on-target sentences and paragraphs. It just doesn't work that way.

When you write, your fingers need to be in sync with your mind.

Concentration equals accomplishment.

But extended periods of intense concentration are somewhat difficult to achieve. Inevitably, other thoughts come to mind as competing demands are placed on your time. That's another advantage of writing in short segments.

Anyone of average intelligence can sustain a concentrated effort for a mere 10 minutes at a time. That's all it takes. You can deal with the other distractions in between. But while you're at it, don't let anything get in your way. Finish off the sub-section you're working on before entertaining the thought of doing anything else.

Focused attention makes your writing come alive. Not only do the words flow freely, the result packs a punch with its impact and ability to communicate.

Write As Fast As You Can

Obviously, you want to get your book finished as quickly as possible and writing as fast as you can shortens the span from concept to completion. Write one segment at a fierce pace and it energizes you. You'll quite naturally want to repeat the process to see if you can do it again. Keep at it and what began as a single segment could in rapid succession turn into another completed chapter.

Writing fast is exhilarating. A wonderful feeling of achievement pours over you as each small section of your book is completed. What began as a huge goal turns into nothing but a collection of 5 – 10 minute writing sessions.

Additionally, writing at a fast clip produces superior material. Try it and you'll see. The faster you write – the better the result. So get it down as quickly as you possibly can and reap a multitude of terrific benefits! I learned this technique from writer and trainer, Steve Manning and it's changed my whole approach.

"The faster you write, the better it is" -- Steve Manning

When you're talking, you don't stop to think about each and every word. You don't give a second thought to sentence structure or paragraph length. You simply speak to communicate... to persuade... to get your message across to the other person in the most unmistakable and effective way.

That's exactly what you want to do when you write. But if you write slowly, you can't possibly keep up as your mind races miles ahead of our fingertips.

Even the fastest fingers in the world can't keep up to speed of the human brain, but nimble fingers tend to create highly readable material.

Whatever writing method you prefer, keep writing at a rapid pace. Allow your thoughts to express themselves through your fingers. Communication should be your mission. Just get it down in the most efficient and direct manner you can on the fly.

Initially this idea might seem crazy to you. If you're like most people, you learned to carefully choose your words, formulate complete sentences and organize individual thoughts into paragraphs. Then it was on to the re-writing phase. Maybe that's why you hated writing assignments in school.

Writing your book fast drowns out those pesky rules that play on relentlessly in the back of your mind. The only voice you hear is your own as the words come to you fast and furiously. The result is quality content created quickly.

How can this be? Well... you're simply communicating your ideas conversationally. What you get is real language with a vibrancy all its own.

There's another obvious advantage to writing as fast as you can. Your book will be completed and on the market that much sooner. I've yet to meet the writer who prefers to postpone profit.

Wipe Out "Writer's Block"

Adequate preparation generates continuous production. When you plan your project, create a detailed map and write in short, timed intervals, you never run out of material to write about – until your book is finished. "Writer's block fails to exist when writing time is preceded by preparation.

Plan your work and then work your plan.

Your outline reveals what you want to say in each segment – and in what order you want to say it. Do your thinking and information gathering at the outline stage.

Outlining presents and organizes your key information in a clear, coherent and logical order. So when it comes down to the writing phase, it's easy as pie. You simply tackle one small section at a time and write for the assigned time period. Then you tackle another segment. This way you're never left staring at a blank monitor wondering what to write next. So this common symptom of "writer's block" will never again happen to you.

Economize on Words

Who says your book has to be 300 pages? That's really not
necessary – especially in today's changing publishing
environment. You can do well with a much shorter volume.

My books have typically ranged from about 80 to 250 pages
in length. If you're anywhere near the 100 page range –
particularly if it's your first book -- you're totally fine for the
printed book market and you can get by with a lot less if
you're going digital. If you plan to sell your creation as an
ebook, a 30 – 50 page product can easily become a bestseller.

Don't fall into the trap of thinking you must have several
hundred pages for your product to officially qualify as a real
book. The winds of change have tossed aside the old
standards – at least in terms of digital books.

If your book turns out to be less than 50 pages, I suggest
going primarily digital. But if you're closer to 100 pages or
more, you've got something that can be marketed in any or
all formats.

Some buyers equate page count with value. Thankfully, many
do not. In the world of e-readers like the Kindle, page
numbers aren't shown and therefore are largely insignificant.

How many times have you read a 400+ page book that could
have been reduced to just 200 pages? Sure, a beefy volume
looks as though it contains more information... and this does
appeal to some readers to be sure. But I tend to subscribe to
the theory that says today's buyer wants the very best
information, delivered in the most expedient way.

If you can say it all in one hundred pages, do so. Loading
your book with filler is a disservice to readers who want and
need your information now.

Keep it lean and mean with valuable information on every page. By doing so, you're showing a healthy respect for the buyer's time. Few people buy non-fiction books to be entertained beside the fireplace for hours on end. **What they do buy is information.** Give it to them quickly, efficiently and without the add-ons that only bulk-up the product and you'll keep the majority of your readers happy.

Make a Habit of Writing

Waiting for perfect planetary alignment or until the spirit moves you before sit down to write will guarantee you never get your book finished. The people who make great strides in the world are those who take action regardless of circumstances and challenges.

There's always something else you could be doing at any given moment in time. That's why it's vital to make your book a priority in your life. Make it a must and don't let anything or anyone deter you. When it's that important to you – you'll get it done.

If you lack the inner resolve to see your project through despite everything else that may be going on in your life, chances are you'll never get it done. If you do, it will take many months, perhaps years to finally complete your book project. Everyone has other "stuff" going on in their lives. Some have more of it to deal with than others, but no one is immune to those issues they would rather not have to deal with at all. That's just the way it is. If you want to get your book written fast, you've got to press on anyway.

When you first get started, set aside a regular time to write. This keeps you moving towards your goal with each passing day. But don't limit your writing time to this designated slot and nothing more.

Once you become deeply involved with your book, you'll find yourself thinking about it at various times of the day. It's a sure sign you've made your writing project a priority.

Seize the moment whenever you can and convert them into productive writing time and you'll feel a wonderful sense of accomplishment. It's particularly gratifying when you can fit a segment or two in unexpectedly.

At work, consider writing through part of your lunch, coffee breaks, while commuting by public transit, or waiting for your car to warm up.

When you're early for an appointment, or waiting to meet a friend at the mall, take advantage of the opportunity to advance another step or two towards completion.

Have you ever written anything while exercising? If not, by all means, give it a try. There's something magical about the creative process of putting words to paper with blood coursing through your veins and your heart beating faster.

Try recording your thoughts into a tape recorder while on a treadmill, exercise bike, or stair-stepper. The trick is to "write" while exercising at a moderate level – one at which you can still speak and remain reasonably coherent. It's a great way to dust off the cobwebs and bring your words, intuition and vision together.

Involve yourself fully in your book and you'll notice pockets of opportunity that you may not have noticed before. Reach out and grab them as they appear. Write another section whenever you've got a few spare moments and you'll feel a sense of gratification about your unplanned "express" progress.

Train Your Mind

Getting yourself moving productively can be difficult in the beginning. But it gets easier as you renew forgotten habits of productivity. Dragging yourself out of the old familiar rut tends to trigger an internal battle in the mind as you weigh the immediate benefits of staying in your "comfort zone" against the long term payoff of having written a successful book and generating extra income on autopilot.

Habits make it easy.

When you're in the habit of writing every day, you don't have to stop and think about it. Schedule your daily writing at the same time every day helps establish the habit. Write every day for a week and it's ten times easier to do the same the next week. When writing becomes a habit, there's no mental tug-of-war. It's almost as easy to get up and start writing as it used to be to hit the snooze button and stay in bed.

Discipline helps get you started. Repetition helps make it routine. When you get to the point where you no longer question it, productivity soars.

Deadlines work wonders in getting past indecision and inaction. When you decide your book will be written in the next 30 days – you set the wheels in motion.

The only thing between where you now stand and the successful completion of your book is action. A series of action steps – specifically, writing several small segments – one after another eventually leads to your finished book.

With an approaching deadline and no means of retreat – you're driven into action. When your back is against the wall, there's only one way to go.

Write The Way You Speak

Writing is simply a form of communication. Your task as a non-fiction writer is to communicate information about your topic in the most direct way possible. When you write conversationally, you write much faster.

Too many first time authors get hung up on the writing part. Don't let this trip you up – it's really quite easy and a ton of fun.

If you have any hesitations about your ability to put words to paper, I'm willing to bet that your early education left an scar on your consciousness concerning writing. Unless you were an exceptional student, you may have got it wrong more often than right at school.

There were all those rules to remember. Books studied were all of the fiction variety, carefully composed by some of the finest writers the world has ever known. I know that if I so much as attempted to write like that I'd only drive myself crazy. Thankfully, I don't have to.

In the nonfiction arena, book buyers want information and they want it in the most direct, clear, understandable and actionable steps possible. You don't need to be able to write flowery prose. In nonfiction, such composition would only get in the way of the message.

All you really need to do is write the way you speak. In fact, forget that you're writing at all. Instead, see yourself as a subject expert with a barrel full if inside knowledge to share with an interested and hungry audience.

Communicate what you know. Share your insights, secrets, techniques and discoveries as though you were discussing these with an interested friend or colleague. Let your words flow naturally, unrestricted by the rules of grammar and written language.

Forget the stilted, stuffy and formal approach in an attempt to write in a "proper" manner. You no longer need the approval of any teacher. No one is ready to pounce on every little thing. You only need to deliver the goods to your audience in a way they can truly appreciate and understand. So just say write it the way you'd say it. You'll be surprised how effective your words are when you record them on paper the same way you would express them verbally.

Share what you've learned in the most direct and down to earth way. Write your words to help a friend understand how to do something. Be as expressive, enthusiastic and animated on paper as you would share your ideas, thoughts, and discoveries in person. Genuine, heartfelt and direct expression is far more important than grammar school rules.

Chunk It Down

Writing a full-size book can be made much easier by breaking it down into smaller components. That's exactly what an outline does for you. Instead of a single 100 page volume -- think of it as ten chapters of ten pages each. When you look at each chapter, don't think of it as 10 pages you need to write, consider it only as ten individual segments that can be written with ease – one at a time – in only 5 or 10 minutes each.

So instead of one 100-page book, you've got 10 chapters of 10 segments each. In other words, all you have to do is write 100 small sections – key bits of information you want to share with your reader – and you're done.

The whole key to tackling what might seem like a large project at the outset is to chunk it down into smaller pieces.

Breaking it down organizes your material in logical fashion, making your presentation much easier for the reader to sail through and find value within. It also makes the writing much faster by simplifying the process and allowing you to put your total energy into one small piece of the puzzle at a time. Refining and organizing your information makes the writing process far easier and more fun.

Get Passionate About Your Subject

Want to make the entire writing process a breeze? Here's how: renew your passion for your subject. If you've lost touch with your topic, it's time to get reacquainted. It won't be long until your passion and zeal shines through again.

Maybe stamp collecting was a hobby you fancied years ago... and that's something you'd love to write about. The first thing you should do is to locate your old collections and lose stamps. Then spend a few afternoons reliving the memories. Flip through the pages of stamp albums. Savor the unique scent of stamps and envelopes from decades gone by. Pretty soon you'll reconnect with the enthusiasm and passion you once had for stamp collecting.

Whatever your subject, make it something you're genuinely interested and passionate about. Not only will the words automatically come to you, they'll flow more freely with a natural rhythm and grace unachievable through forced writing.

You want satisfied readers... readers who will recommend your book to their friends. Reader contentment can only be achieved when your ideas are accepted -- when they have fully bought into your message.

Being genuine, passionate and interested in your topic is the best way to "sell" readers on your ideas. True enthusiasm is authentic and sincere. Words are more descriptive and vibrant when your information is expressed enthusiastically. Demonstrating a sincere interest in your subject matter helps to strengthen the bond between reader and writer.

Ignore the Censor

Finding your true voice and writing effortlessly means freeing yourself of the critic and censor inside. Stick to your sub-topic and keep writing as fast as you can. Once you're engaged in writing, don't stop until the timer sounds.

Avoid re-reading what you've just written. Don't question what you've put down on the page. Instead, trust that you've expressed yourself clearly and succinctly. Don't fret about the language used. Just get the words out and let them flow.

If you want to maximize productivity and turn out pages of quality content quickly and easily, ignore the tendency to censor your message. Just say what's on your mind and record those exact thoughts on the page. Leave the editing for later.

Keep advancing towards the objective. Stick with it for the allotted time on each section. Communicate from the heart as passionately and persuasively as you can.

Give yourself permission to write whatever you want.

Remove the barricades and just write like there's no tomorrow. You'll quickly find your true voice and allow it to communicate most effectively. You'll astonish yourself with the material you create when the self-imposed shackles of limitation are finally removed.

Trust Yourself

It can happen at any time from the conception stage... to outlining... even during the writing of your book. It's that moment when you start to question yourself. Is this good enough? Do I have enough material here? Is this what my reader really wants and needs?

Writing your first book is a new experience. You've never done anything quite like this before. You want to give it your absolute best, which of course, is the only way to take on any project. Do it to the best of your ability, or don't do it at all. Give your reader every morsel of valuable data and information you've discovered, created and adapted – or don't even bother.

If you do your best at every opportunity, there's no reason to question your capabilities.

Trust yourself to get it done. Know in your heart that the information you have to share is worthwhile and important. It's likely much more valuable to your targeted reader than you realize. Have faith in your inventory of ideas... and your ability to share these effectively.

Trust the Process

If you want to write a terrific, full-size book... and you want to get it completed in the least amount of time possible, I urge you to follow the simple methods laid out here. It works for me -- I know it will work for you too.

These ideas are time-tested and proven beyond doubt. They work... if you work them. If getting your book completed is your goal, the content you've found here will get you there.

You'll have to trust me on this and be willing to take the steps. I can't prove the effectiveness of this process unless you're willing to step up to the plate. No one can do it for you – it takes some initiative and faith on your part.

Look at these ideas from a purely logical point of view.

Planning is a logical prerequisite to the efficient accomplishment of any objective. If you gather your information and organize it from the beginning, the task of writing your book is much easier. I think I've hammered home this point quite enough already.

Divide the large goal of a book into individual steps. Consider the 10 to 20 most important ideas relating to the overall concept or thesis. Make these your chapters.

Then with each chapter, break it down to individual segments of ½-page to 2 pages each – whatever it takes to say what needs to be said about that segment.

When you look at your giant book project as nothing more than a series of tiny segments, it's not such a big deal after all.

I'm here to tell you that there's really no mystery to writing your own nonfiction book. If I can do it – anyone can. Just follow along from step A-B-C and so on... and your book will be 100% complete – in no time at all.

Get to the Juicy Stuff Immediately

Forget the filler. Banish the balderdash. Wipe out any wind-up. Just deliver the genuine goods and present your best material right out of the gate.

Focus on giving your reader the juiciest of secrets from the start. Do this and readers will instantly recognize and appreciate the value of your book. They'll value gaining access to some of your best material, without wading through pages of non-essential details of lesser import.

Writing in time-limited segments forces you to prioritize your ideas and express the most significant concepts immediately. With only minutes to cover a sub-topic, there's no holding back. Jump in and get right to the essential information.

Start with the most significant fact pertaining to each sub-topic. Then proceed to the next most important fact, until your time is up for that particular segment.

It's an "inverted pyramid" or "funnel" approach where you begin with the biggest, most valuable and important idea and write your way through a short list of 3 to 5 ideas per segment. This ensures that you always cover the most significant information by prioritizing the list of details.

Should time run out before you're done writing, you have a choice to make. You could extend the time to cover additional ideas... you could "red-flag" the section to go back later and reassess... or you could simply finish the sentence and move on to the next segment. I've used all three options at varying times -- depending on the specifics.

When you write as fast as you can and you know you've only got a few minutes before moving, it forces you to prioritize. After a while, your brain gets used to generating golden ideas immediately.

You don't have time to create a scenario, or build up to a grand revelation. You're forced to unveil the best information first. Additionally, as you nail down the details most beneficial to the reader, more grand ideas enter into your consciousness. It's as though you've tapped into a rich source of intelligence and all you have to do is keep those fingers moving to capitalize on it.

Do Something Everyday

Develop a "bias for action" as Brain Tracy, author of Maximum Achievement suggests. Get in the habit of working on your book. Take steps forward – even baby steps count. Follow through with enough small steps at regular intervals and your book will be completed before you know it.

Any action towards completion advances you forward. Look for those opportunities to turn down time into another written segment or two. You'll enjoy a sense of accomplishment that satisfies the soul... and you'll be that much closer to your goal.

There's always something you could be doing to accelerate the completion of your book. Make full use of email to interview experts. Email is completely unobtrusive, yet it can serve you 24 hours a day.

Having trouble sleeping? Why waste your time tossing and turning? Get up, write a few segments and then go back to bed. You'll wake up ahead of schedule and you'll have marched a few more steps closer towards the goal line.

Chapter 10: Chapter: From Rough Draft to Polished Book

Use Your Outline to Build a Table of Contents

Once you've written your planned chapters and segments, it's time to take what you have and polish it up.

If you've followed the system thus far, creating a table of contents is quick and easy. Since you've already prepared an outline, you're more than halfway towards a completed table of contents too. Not only does your outline serve as a framework for your book, it's also the foundation of your Table of Contents section.

The organization of your ideas is already done. All you need to do at this stage is adjust your outline to make it a more accurate, descriptive and perhaps enticing framework of your written material.

To start, copy and paste your outline at the beginning of your document. If your outline is hand-written, you'll need to convert it now to typed copy. Simply take your exact headings used in the outline and list them in the order presented. You'll probably make some minor adjustments to your sequence, enabling a smoother, more logical or practical presentation of your information.

At this point you've got a basic table of contents. Now it's time to improve upon it.

Take each of your subject topics and make it more appealing to potential readers and readers alike. Make it exciting, intriguing and interesting. Like a headline, your chapter titles have the power to draw your target audience inside.

Here are a few random chapter topics/subtopics from published table of contents pages:

From: The 4-Hour Workweek (Timothy Ferriss)

Rules That Change The Rules: Everything Popular is Wrong
The End of Time Management: Illusions and Italians
Interrupting Interruption and the Art of Refusal
Mini Retirements: Embracing the Mobile Lifestyle
The Top 13 New Rich Mistakes

From: Jumpstart Your Business Brain (Doug Hall)

How To Triple Effectiveness of Salespeople, Advertising and Marketing Efforts
How To Craft A Dramatic Difference
The Science Behind Capitalist Creativity
How To Fuel Your Brain For Maximum Productivity
Multiply Your Brain By Borrowing Others

From: Zero Limits (Joe Vitale)

Finding The World's Most Unusual Therapist
The Shocking Truth About Intentions
How To Create Results Faster
Cigars, Hamburgers, and Killing The Divine
The Truth Behind The Story

Your table of contents can help you sell more books. Not only does it reveal specific content, it helps "sell" readers on the valuable information contained between the covers.

In a bookstore environment, books that sell capture attention of potential buyers who then take a closer look. Beyond the front and back covers, the next most logical place for prospective buyers to look is the table of contents. A powerful table of contents can be equally effective as an enclosure in direct mail packages, or as a separate page on a website.

Review each chapter topic with the idea and intention of making it more powerful and alluring. But don't stop there. Carry this thinking through to each sub-topic of each chapter. The more marketing appeal you can work into your titles and sub-titles, the more appeal your book will enjoy in the marketplace.

Synchronize Your Table of Contents and Text

Take your freshly composed rough draft and reorganize it to make what you've written much more logical and coherent. The last thing you want to do is interrupt the flow once writing has commenced. But there's a good chance that even your best efforts to prioritize and format material at the outline stage can be enhanced after the written details have been filled in.

Take a look at each chapter with fresh eyes.

Adjust your presentation accordingly for maximum impact and understanding. Re-evaluate the sequential order of your sub-topics. Make item number one the first step in the process... most important specific sub-topic... first to occur chronologically... or the most general sub-topic from the list. Follow this with item number two – the next most logical sub-topic. Carry on this process for each chapter to ensure a more natural flow.

Rearrange, reformat, or reorganize your details to make each chapter as powerful and reader-friendly as possible. Double check to make sure the sequence listed in your table of contents matches your text exactly.

Eliminate Unnecessary Words

Re-read each segment you've written and keep an eye peeled for extraneous, non-essential details – details that add no real value to your work. Prune your copy to eliminate excess words, sentences, and even paragraphs.

For maximum effect, you want to include the minimum number of words to cover your topic adequately. Insist that each and every word contributes something to your overall message. Filling up pages isn't the objective. Sharing key information of value is what writing a successful non-fiction book is about.

Deliver your information to the reader in the most direct way. Strive for clarity and instant comprehension. Make it easy for the reader to read and understand your words and examples. Trim the fat. Anything that doesn't add meaning to the message should be deleted. Anything that aids understanding and provides for a more direct exchange of information should remain. Make every word earn its keep.

While writing, you may not have at your fingertips specific examples, anecdotes, or case histories you wanted to share with reader. Never let it slow you down. Simply mark the section where your example would be a good fit and carry on writing. I use <brackets> to indicate missing material requiring follow up. This works well as it flags the segment in question, making finding it later much easier.

As you re-read your draft, fill in any blanks as you encounter them. Plug the holes with rich supporting material.

New opportunities to deliver helpful examples, expert quotations, or stories tend to appear. Inserting relevant support material adds dimension to your work, making it more readable and effective at driving home the salient points.

Add details as they come to mind while you continue to edit. It's easy to go back and plug in any holes after you've written 100+ pages.

Stress Key Points Using Tools of Emphasis

Your title, chapter titles, even sub-titles act as headlines. As such, they should be clearly identified. Headings command a place of visual prominence. The most dominant "headline" is of course, your book's title. As such, it should be set in large size type on the front cover – clearly distinguished from everything else. The next largest type size should be reserved for chapter titles, followed by the sub-titles that fall under each chapter title.

There's a simple reason for setting headings in larger, bold type: it prioritizes and organizes information in a visual sense, making it easier for the reader to understand.

Your title should reveal the overall subject matter covered. Each chapter covers the key elements pertaining to the subject and each sub-title highlights one significant concept relating to that chapter.

Headings are an obvious tool of emphasis, but many more exist. Asterisks are effective in footnoting related details that don't necessarily fit into the text. Bold typefaces, indented paragraphs, underlined or italicized text clearly call out to the reader to emphasize key points.

Text boxes are particularly effective at highlighting key point summaries or as a visual reinforcement of a particularly important point the author wants to make.

Numbered and bulleted lists add visual relief and eye appeal, making these great choices for formulas, step-by-step summaries, or itemized listings.

Check For Obvious Breaks In Continuity

Editing is essentially an exercise in polishing your writing before publishing your book. You want to make it as good as can be, without expanding the editing phase into a long, laborious drawn out exercise that takes you weeks or months to complete.

You want to get your book completed and out in the marketplace so other people can begin to get the benefit of your ideas too. So clean it up as best you can, but don't let an imperfect book postpone your profits.

Apart from the obvious spelling mistakes and grammatical inconsistencies, you also need to edit for comprehension. Make sure you stay on track, with one idea following another in a way that makes sense to readers. You want it to flow in a natural way, merging one thought with the next and organizing your sub-topics in a way that makes it easy for the reader to get exactly what you're saying.

Each segment should be quick to read and understand within minutes. This is easy to accomplish when you write in time-limited segments. Using this method, there's actually very little editing to do. But you do want to be sure that ideas discussed under each title, relate directly to the sub-topic.

Add Additional Components

Upon completion of the writing phase, you'll be left with many pages of standard text, most of which assumes a similar format. Chapters tend to run about the same length as do most individual segments.

It's always a good idea to add a little flair to your book with a few simple additions. Your table of contents was the first edition to those standard pages of text. You can easily add others as well. Following is a list of possible sections you might want to consider adding to your book. Use whatever seems to be a good fit for your book.

Bibliography
About The Author
End of Product Catalogue
Transcribed Interviews of Experts
Recommended Resources
Bonus Chapters or Reports
Key Idea Summary
Practical Exercise or Action Plan
Templates

Find One More Key Idea

Stretch You Mind. Go beyond what you've already shared in each chapter. Reach deep into your back of tricks and pull out one more gem you can share with your readers.

Think you've exhausted your resources? Review your list of sub-topics as you review each chapter. Ask yourself... What else is crucial here? What additional inside secret can I share with my reader to enhance her experience and add to the value of my book?

Give yourself 60 seconds to come up with one extra bit of information or helpful advice that can make this particular chapter that much better.

Next, add a few key words and perhaps a fresh new example to bring it home. Then, spend the next 5 - 10 minutes writing this additional segment. If you thought you had a good chapter before doing this, you'll be delighted when you make it that much better.

Try it. You may not uncover new gems for every single chapter, but you'll add enough extra value to make your book that much better.

Simple Layout Techniques

Strive for a simple style. Anything that aids readability is a good thing. Regular headings help the reader sort through your material and categorize it. It also makes for reading in bite-size pieces – something anyone can do in just a few spare minutes.

Keep your paragraphs relatively short – it's much more inviting that way. Avoid those extra long paragraphs that can span the better part of a page. Make your book light and breezy and there's a much greater chance buyers will actually read it.

Stick with "left-aligned" text. This is the default setting on virtually all text programs for a good reason: it's the most readable of all. It's the way we all learned to read – start from the top left corner of the page and move to the right.

Left alignment maintains a constant starting point on the left side of the page – a reference or guideline if you will. If you've ever tried reading more than a paragraph of centered or right-aligned text, you know how annoying it can be.

Consider the venue you're publishing and format your book accordingly.

Generally, narrow columns make quicker and easier reading. If your text spans the full width of a standard 8.5 x 11 inch page, it's mentally exhausting and hard on the eyes. White space provides a rest area for the eyes, so do allow for adequate space, particularly on the left and right side of the page. Some print books layouts provide a separate column on the right for the reader to make notes.

One final step is to add page numbers.

It's a simple thing to do in most programs and it's important in print or PDF formats. On the Kindle publishing platform, page numbers are irrelevant for the most part. But don't forget this important detail if you're publishing print or PDF versions of your book. It's always nice to have easily identifiable points of reference and nothing beats numbered pages for quickly locating important details.

Check Your Words

Read through your book while keeping an eye out for spelling mistakes. Don't rely on the spell-check option that comes with your word processing package. Use it, if you wish... but never trust it entirely.

It's easy to insert the incorrect version of a word. I've used "your" when I really meant to write "you're"... or "to", when it should have been "too". It's an easy thing to do and it seems that no matter how many times I edit my work, the occasional error still sneaks through. But if I relied entirely on my spell-checker, those errors would surely multiply. It merely checks spelling – not spelling related to context. So use whatever word processing program you have, but don't forget that this is only one step.

Simple, conversational English is an effective way to communicate. So be on the lookout for fancy words – words you wouldn't generally use in everyday conversation. You want your book to be read and understood by all your readers. It's not a demonstration of vocabulary – it's a means of communicating your ideas to help the reader solve a problem or achieve a goal. Write it the way you'd say it - that's always a good way to go.

Design a Cover

A well-designed cover can make a difference in your results. It's this finishing touch that adds colour, character and identity to your creation. A simple cover ties together a bunch of typed pages and turns them into something much more valuable. Adding a cover to your book is something you'll want to do with any publishing platform you choose.

In bookstores, it's usually the title and cover that catches the eye of buyers.

Once a book is in the hands of a potential buyer, the cover speaks volumes. It conveys subtleties, nuances and information beyond those expressed by mere words.

In a catalogue setting, a cover adds a visual element and dimension.

On a website, it's the same thing. Printed covers are also effective marketing tools. I've seen them used as package inserts and direct mail pieces, as well as enclosures submitted with press releases. A good cover captures eyeballs. Use it to your advantage.

Anyone can design a basic cover. If you don't have the tools to create a digital version, create a sketch and take it to desktop publisher. It might even help to employ coloured pencils in the process and choose specific shades you want on the finished product. If you can afford to hire a skilled graphic artist, that's an even better option. If you plan to sell your books through stores, getting some outside help with your cover design makes good business sense.

If you choose to create your own cover, here are a few simple tips to turn a basic idea into an attractive cover:

- Place your title in big, bold text
- Make the title as large as can be, without separating any words
- Insert the sub-title close to the main title, but set the sub-title in smaller type, perhaps in a different style or font
- Add your name as author towards the bottom of the page
- Take each element (title, sub-title & author's name) and align them uniformly by using the same starting point for each element by creating an imaginary line that links all 3 components together
- Add a graphic enhancement – photograph, sketch, or customized clip art
- Try various color combinations until you've got a winner
- Adjust the components until you're satisfied with the finished product

You can do it all on your computer if you're so inclined and have the software capability. The cheapest option I've found is the Open Office Drawing program. It's a free download and gives you decent flexibility with typefaces, fonts, colors and images. If you're comfortable with another program, that's what you should be using. If you would rather have someone else handle the details of cover design, that's the route you should go.

For print books, you'll want to also include a back cover that does an effective job of selling readers on your book.

Start with a headline that's a natural extension of your title and sub-title combination. Then, think of the biggest, most compelling benefits your book offers and list these as bullet points. If you've managed to get some reviews or early testimonials, include these on your back cover. Another option is an "About the Author" section.

Ideally, you want a back cover that speaks to your target reader in an irresistible way about all the potential advantages your book offers.

It's also important to maintain a sense of continuity in style, color and design. Make your back cover look as though it belongs.

Beginning and Ending

Introductions set the stage by preparing the reader for the information that follows. So it's usually a good idea to include this section. An effective introduction provides an overview of the entire book. It's the "Reader's Digest" or "TV Guide" version – a short, concise guide or preview that makes the reader want more.

Invite the reader along on your journey. Inspire them to accomplish what you have and more. Fuel reader enthusiasm and build a sense of anticipation. Let them know in no uncertain terms that they too can learn and apply your secrets quickly, easily and decisively.

A good introduction should sell the reader on reading your book. Enlighten readers about the value they hold in their hands. Reassure them that contained within those very pages is the precise information they seek to get wherever they want to go. Remind readers of the payoff that lies just around the corner.

Add a copyright notice right after your cover page. Clearly indicate exclusive ownership of your book. List the year of publication, your name, and company name if you have one and choose to list it as publisher. Copyright protection won't prevent theft, particularly if you publish a digital version of your book. But it does act as a deterrent and will at least stop those with at least some sense of right and wrong.

Your copyright page is a mere technical formality to be sure. But it's an important page -- one you should always include in your book.

Finish your book off with a concluding chapter. It needn't be lengthy or particularly detailed. But what it should do is bring your message in for a smooth landing.

Capture the essence of your major message. Summarize key points. Help the reader take each individual chapter and relate it to the whole.

Your concluding chapter should help crystallize the information already digested by the reader. It's a reminder of major lessons learned and a status report of where the reader stands now. Make the reader feel good about her new found knowledge and freshly acquired skills.

End the last sentence of the last chapter of your book with power. You've come full circle, explaining in detail all the reader needs to know. Simply end your text with the one word or combination of words that best describes the theme of your book and the OUTCOME the reader wants. Sum it up succinctly.

Choose a word that fits your project best. Here are a few words that could work: Freedom, Money, Riches, Optimum Health, Weight Loss, Success, Unconditional Love, Getting Organized, timesaver, lifesaver, etc. Whatever your topic – choose an appropriate key word to wrap up your book.

Next, insert your concluding key word at the bottom of a blank page... and simply fill in the details. Before writing, place your table of contents in front of you. The reason for this is to have a clear overview of the text you're about to summarize. Set your timer for seven minutes and craft your final chapter down to the last word.

Readers will marvel at your writing ability. More importantly, they'll be left with a wonderful feeling of satisfaction.

Closing Thoughts

Writing a book is a life-transforming experience. But the only way to fully convince you of this is to get you to experience the joys of authorship for yourself.

I've given you all you need to get it done – in far less time too. But whether you profit from this information or not is ultimately up to you.

It's been said that everyone has a book in them. I agree. Your book can pay off in so many ways that it's plain crazy not to pursue this full speed ahead. I know writing and self-publishing my first book changed my life forever... and I'm willing to bet it will change yours too.

In these pages I've covered the important details and shared my experience to help you get it done. But if there's anything I've left out... or if there's any way I can help you personally, I'm happy to do so and would love to hear from you by email.

If you always though writing a book would take months or even years to complete, you now know that's just not the case. What you have here is a system for writing a real book of 100 to 200 pages – and getting it done in a matter of days.

I can't guarantee that you'll sell a million copies, or make a million dollars, although I sincerely hope you do.

What I can tell you is that if you follow my guidance and write the book that's inside you, you will own an asset that can generate cash month after month, year after year.

When you write a book, you do the work once. But you get paid thousands of times over. What's more is... you're genuinely helping people solve their problems. There's no better feeling in the world than to serve others by providing information of value through the written word.

Get started now and write your book. All it takes is one small decision. But that decision can open the floodgates to a lifetime of rich rewards.

Free Bonus

Please contact me by email and I'll provide you with a free bonus gift of 1300 "power words" to help you kick-start your segment writing, or to give you additional creative ideas should you ever get stuck. Enjoy and... happy book writing to you!

Robert Boduch
http://bizpofitbuilder.com/
rboduch@rogers.com